**A Bite-Sized Lifestyle Book**

# Alfa Male
## …If you're brave enough?

## Stuart Haining ACIB, MCIM

Published by Bite-Sized Books Ltd 2019
©Stuart Haining 2019

The moral right of Stuart Haining to be identified as the author of this work has been asserted by him in accordance with the Copyright, Designs and Patents Act 1988

ISBN: 9781686274749

Second Edition December 2019

**BITE-SIZED BOOKS**

Bite-Sized Books Ltd Cleeve Road, Goring RG8 9BJ UK
information@bite-sizedbooks.com
**Registered in the UK. Company Registration No: 9395379**

# Biography

Stuart Haining is a serial entrepreneur, runs an innovative carbon-neutral Online Marketing Agency, and not surprisingly is a fan of good design – a passion he has carried through to his car ownership.

Until recently, his *day-car* was a 420 bhp V8 4.7 litre Aston Martin Vantage (the subject of two Bite Sized Lifestyle Books, one about the practicalities of acquiring and running such a prestige vehicle, the other about the pitfalls of parting with his much cherished Supercar).

But Stuart's *long-journey* car (due to great fuel economy) is a 2.4 litre V5 Alfa Romeo Brera SV with a mere 210 bhp, the latest in a long line of Alfas, soon to be replaced by a more powerful Guilia, Stelvio or Quadrifoglio. So it's probably true to say that with almost 20 years of continuous ownership, the Alfa marque lies even closer to his heart.

This latest Bite-Sized book aims to dispel a few myths about these often quirky cars, not least that you don't need to be a male to own an Alfa or even particularly brave, especially now that rust, breakdowns and sky-high depreciation are pretty much a thing of the past, provided you take ownership seriously and carefully of course, and we'll hopefully help you navigate through all that with this informative and humorous book.

**Paul Davies, Editor, Bite-Sized Books Limited**

# Author's Warning

The title of this Bite-Sized Book Alfa Male has been selected as word play suitable for a book title rather than as an serious commentary about Alfa Romeo cars being a male preserve with no females allowed, or inferring that only men are brave.....I think child-birth already puts that idea firmly to bed! Whilst most sporty vehicles globally are indeed purchased by men, recent Alfa models such as the Mito and Giulietta are particularly popular with females (who actually accounted for 45% of all Alfa sales in 2012) and have helped balance the marque's gender split since. These days all Alfas are of course suitable for almost anyone to drive and you probably don't even need to be that brave to own one either!

# Contents

Biography
Author's Warning
Introduction
Chapter 1.
    Love at First Sight?
Chapter 2.
    My Driving Credentials
Chapter 3.
    The Test Drive & Shopping Around
Chapter 4.
    Not Like Other Cars
Chapter 5.
    Awaiting Delivery
Chapter 6.
    Snagging & First Impressions
Chapter 7.
    The Driving Experience
Chapter 8.
    Pimp My Ride?
Chapter 9.
    The Garages
Chapter 10.
    Problems Encountered
Chapter 11.
    Misnomers
Chapter 12.
    The Truisms
Chapter 13.
    Living with Alfa Romeo
Chapter 14.
    Running Costs

Chapter 15.
    Depreciation
Chapter 16.
    Selling the Wheels
Chapter 17.
    Owner Loyalty
Chapter 18.
    Whatever Next?
Chapter 19.
    Would I recommend an Alfa?
Chapter 20.
    Hints & Tips.
Chapter 21.
    Summary
Footnote
*Bite-Sized Lifestyle Books*
*Bite-Sized Books Catalogue*

# Introduction

If you've ever owned an Alfa Romeo you'll probably be only too familiar with an annoyingly frequent experience when you first tell people what car you chose to drive. All too often they'll say, firstly, "*Gosh, you're* **brave**" only to follow up with a quip like "*Don't they* **rust** *on sight?*" The particularly annoying pundit may even follow through with a comment about "*regular* **breakdowns**" or "*sky-high* **depreciation**" rates. So it's easy to wonder why Alfa Romeo have such passionate supporters, of which I am very much one myself, and I'm not alone. Or am I?

Any avid watchers of programs like **Top Gear** will be all too familiar at seeing Alfa Romeo score in the middle of the score-board in the various driving tests yet only to be awarded the surprise final gold star when it's time for the presenters to get off-the-fence and say which car they'd actually prefer to own if they could only pick **one** – it's **almost always the Alfa Romeo that wins**.

And indeed alongside my beloved Aston Martin they make up one of the very few brands to make a **regular appearance on the Top Gear Cool Wall,** and even occasionally the **Sub Zero** section – but to my knowledge have **never yet been rated as uncool**. PS. If you've never seen Top Gear this is the bit of the show where with much fan-fare they paste up pictures of new cars as they are launched onto a giant wall board split into sections of varying coolness!

Why then do the presenters rarely drive an Alfa themselves? It can only be the persistent belief, maybe even almost a **subconscious** belief for them too, that the good performing car they've just tested within an inch of its life was in fact just a mirage and the truth must be that generally you do indeed still need to brave to own one, due I assume to perceived **hassles, breakdowns and depreciation?**

Having owned a series of different Alfa Romeo models for close to **20 years** continuously, in the process racking up enough miles to circumnavigate the planet **ten times** or get me to the **Moon,** I have experienced very **few headaches** and certainly nothing to warrant the thought that it's a brave purchase decision. Breakdowns have been **rare** and **depreciation manageable** – but this may all be down to how I use my cars.

This book then is an opportunity for you to decide for yourself.

# Chapter 1.

## Love at First Sight?

I come from a family with a passion for nice cars, starting with my grandad who owned a trendy Morgan Sportscar. My dad owned various high performance Jaguars, my mum a couple of then trendsetting Ford Capris, and my half-brother was the proud owner of a Lotus Eclat. It's no surprise then that I liked nice cars too and even if my early models weren't exactly fast, they'd always have a **little something extra in terms of interior or exterior design,** even if I had to add the go-faster stripes myself!

> **Editor's note** – I gather that's a trend that still continues!
>
> **Author's note** – I'm afraid so, my Aston had a hand built leather-covered voltmeter fitted under the dash (so I could keep an eye on the battery) and my Alfa Brera has a few extra Lusso and Design Giugiaro **badges** never intended by the manufacturer! I think they further improve the lines of the design!
>
> You can see for yourself in the Pimp your Ride section of the book!

I think from all this it would be easy to assume that I was well versed in all the main car brands and especially those with a racing pedigree? But nothing could be further from the truth.

Whilst I liked nice design in all things, I wasn't a huge fan of motorsport until my 40's, so that's around the new millennium, and hence I had little knowledge of Alfa Romeo, at least not in a detailed way commensurate with being any kind of fan or supporter – in fact I was largely **ignorant** about them.

Little did I know that here was a brand for which **Enzo Ferrari originally raced** long before building his own car company, and in fact early Alfa race cars carried the Ferrari logo which you can see in a model picture later.

Nor did I know that this marque actually **won the inaugural world championship** for Grand Prix cars. So whilst they weren't a brand quite as aged as say Peugeot or Mercedes, (although Alfa Romeo also date back over a century) with Alfa we have a car brand with arguably the best pedigree around when it comes to building **unusual cars with a slant towards higher-performance**. It's what they've specialised in almost since day one.

But even this alone wasn't enough for me to take notice or consider buying an Alfa. For that we first needed a bit of **peer pressure.**

- *So the Alfa brand probably first came to my attention when the boss of an advertising agency that I worked closely with acquired a shiny new executive saloon. A Alfa 164 in red. It was very smart with a super interior. I admired him a lot personally and trusted his business judgement completely so I started to think 'if Alfa was good enough for him, maybe it was good enough for me to aspire to one day too?' The first seed was sown.*
- *Said seed quickly had a bit of water added when just a few weeks later a work colleague at a similar grade to me but in a different Marketing Department also acquired an Alfa, this time a 155 GTA. And he loved this car so much he apparently used to get togged out in special clothes just for the pleasure of washing and polishing his car inside his*

*garage. And even I don't do things that unusual. It was odd but certainly another mark in the marques favour (pun intended).*

> **Editor's note** – I thought everybody used the local illegal car wash for a £fiver?
>
> **Author's note** – I don't – that's £5 wasted plus I need the exercise. And anyway, this predates Polish car washes or car washers that also polish!

- The final straw came when one of the Account Managers for an even larger London Advertising Agency, with whom I also worked closely, very excitedly invited me out to the company car park to see the new car which her grateful bosses had just **treated her** to, due to her success in winning new business by the £m. She apparently was advised she could choose almost any car. And yes, you've guessed it, she also picked an Alfa, this time a Series **4 Spider** 2000, sadly that's not the boat-tailed one! But it really was a stunning car, and red of course with a tan leather interior, Wow.

So whilst my love affair with Alfa Romeo wasn't instant, in fact it took a while to mature, by now with three supposedly sensible people whose opinions I trusted all buying into this Alfa brand, it was time to **add it to my shopping list** when I was ready to get my next new car.

Needless to say that might not be immediate or as straightforward as I had hoped as at the time I was the lucky recipient of a company paid-for car. These were only changed every 24 months and they were also very **strict** about which cars you could and couldn't get with your allotted money. And what's the betting (due to that perceived hassle and reliability issue again) that Alfa wouldn't be on the list?

**Editor's note** – So was Alfa on the list of approved cars?

**Author's note** – Of course not. They expected you to get respectably solid cars like a Rover 75. I had previously bucked the trend with a 200 bhp **Rover 220 Coupe** (of which only 350 were hand-made to apparently enable Rover to launch a new race series alongside the Porsche Cup), so that went down well with my bosses as it was a Supercar of its day, like a fast roller skate, and technically it was outside my pay-grade but I managed to work around that!

I followed that up with the first Land Rover Freelander in the company which was technically impossible as that was a new model which 100% was above my grade as an option. I achieved it by taking things out of the standard specification (split rear seat, alloy wheels, spare real wheel etc) and then adding back just enough to get within £5 of my allowance, much to everyone's amazement and annoyance. I wasn't expecting to be so lucky when it came to manipulating the system to get an Alfa on my choices list, and indeed I couldn't.

So for a while my Alfa dream had to stay on hold.

It materialised a few years later when partly fuelled by my desire for a nicer car, I decided to leave my then employer Barclays, raise £2.2m in Venture Capital and start my own business as a technology incubator – inventing and launching a series of crazy new ideas in the hope of coming up with the next Amazon or Facebook type of online innovation. This then was the perfect time to put **Alfa back onto the shopping agenda**, but I still wasn't won over 100% completely. **I still needed fully convincing.**

Before I get into how that final conversion happened let me share a little more about my own particular motoring pedigree as this may give you a little more insight into the kind of driver and owner I am.

# Chapter 2.

## My Driving Credentials.

My first experience of driving, spookily enough, was also **Italian**. At a time when all the teenage lads in school in the 1970's wanted a Fizzer, otherwise known as a Yamaha FS1E moped, I decided to go down a more **exclusive** route, with my parents helping by contributing 50% of the cost.

> NB. The Yamaha were legally classified as mopeds as they had peddles like a push-bike but cleverly the 49cc two-stroke engines were such high compression that it was a powerful, if noisy, engine making them like relatively fast small motorbikes once the peddles were disengaged. Which is what everyone did when they were underage and couldn't qualify to ride a bigger motorbike as a learner or pass a test on a real motorbike. They were supposed to be limited to 30mph, but rarely seemed to be.

The more discerning student went for the slightly less high pitched four stroke engine in a Honda SS50, but in most other regards it was similar to the Yamaha.

I on the other hand had fallen in love with the glorious spaceframe and perfect welding visible externally on the Italian brand of **proper motorcycle** called **Gilera**. These days it's reminiscent to me of seeing the innards on a building like the Shard or Lloyds of London, but back then it was mostly only the Italians who would proudly show off welds and hidden paintwork.

So my first motoring was on a 50CC trials / off-road bike by Gilera, and I seem to recall with a bit of tuning and minus any need for pedals this could achieve close to 70mph. I was in good company too, I subsequently learned that the first ever motorbike to achieve a lap time of 100mph around the Isle of Man TT circuit was a Gilera, albeit a 500, ridden by the famous **Geoff Duke** in the 1950's.

FS1E Yamaha vs Gilera Trials bike. No contest in the beauty parade IMHO.

I had this mini-motorbike for several years before selling up and saving for my first Austin Mini car, it obviously had to be bright red to catch the eye. It was a bargain but an absolute rogue mechanically as it was a former hire car, so please don't ever buy one of those!

Here then is my list of cars owned, private at the top of the chart, company-funded at the bottom.

| | Previous Owners | Value When New | Acquired | Owned For (Months) | Paid | Sold For | Depreciation (Per Annum) | |
|---|---|---|---|---|---|---|---|---|
| Austin Mini | 2 | £ 1,250 | 1978 | 24 | £ 750 | £ 450 | 20.0% | |
| Vauxhall Cavalier Coupe | 1 | £ 3,500 | 1983 | 24 | £ 1,250 | £ 950 | 12.0% | |
| Vauxhall Astra Coupe (New) | 0 | £ 5,000 | 1985 | 48 | £ 4,200 | £ 2,000 | 13.1% | |
| Vauxhall Cavalier Hatchback (New) | 0 | £ 13,000 | 1989 | 48 | £ 11,000 | £ 7,000 | 9.1% | |
| Vauxhall Cavalier Saloon | 1 | £ 10,000 | 1993 | 18 | £ 7,500 | £ 4,500 | 26.7% | |
| Austin Mini | 3 | £ 2,500 | 1995 | 6 | £ 500 | £ 525 | -10.0% | |
| Vauxhall Astra Saloon | 1 | £ 7,000 | 1995 | 12 | £ 1,500 | £ 1,200 | 20.0% | |
| Alfa Romeo 156 Lusso Saloon (New) | 0 | £ 17,000 | 2000 | 107 | £ 15,600 | £ 1,200 | 10.4% | |
| Alfa Romeo GT Coupe | 1 | £ 22,000 | 2009 | 19 | £ 12,500 | £ 8,900 | 18.2% | 13.1% |
| Alfa Romeo Brera SV Coupe (V5) | 1 | £ 27,000 | 2010 | 95 | £ 13,500 | £ 1,850 | 10.9% | |
| Aston Martin V8 Vantage | 1 | £ 120,000 | 2012 | 81 | £ 40,000 | £ 26,000 | 5.2% | |
| **Average - Private Cars** | 1 | £ 20,750 | | 44 | £ 9,845 | £ 4,961 | **13.5%** | |
| | | | | | 47% | 50% | | |
| Rover 220 Coupe | 1 | £ 18,315 | 1996 | 12 | | | | |
| Rover 600 Saloon (New) | 0 | £ 19,000 | 1997 | 24 | | | | |
| Land Rover Freelander (New) | 0 | £ 20,000 | 1999 | 14 | | | | |
| **Overall Average - All Cars** | 0.8 | £ 20,400 | | 38 | | | | |

A few things struck me from looking at this list with a critical eye:

- Firstly, how loyal I have generally been to UK made products – I'm counting Vauxhall as British (as the Astra's were made at Ellesmere Port and most of the Cavaliers at Luton), and obviously the Austin Minis and Rovers were made in the Midlands or Halewood. And the recent Aston Martin was made at Gaydon in Oxfordshire.
- In total I have driven British cars for about 26 years, so around two-thirds of my motoring experiences. With this pedigree it was a big conversion for me to want to jump in the direction of Italy for the other third of my driving. NB. Not shown in this list are the various French, German, Spanish, Czech and Japanese cars I have driven for short periods as rental cars or pool cars at the Bank etc so I do at least have some limited experience of a still wider portfolio too.
- On average my private cars are first acquired at around 47% of the new cost, so they are typically

just falling due for MOT's. And I tend to keep my vehicles for a while – on average around 44 months, so almost 4 years each.
- On average I sell them on for 50% of my purchase price, which equates to 13.5% per annum depreciation cost. This means the previous owners lost 53% in say 3 years whereas in a longer period I lost just 23% in value, so I must strike good deals when both buying and selling? This is probably because I don't generally impulse buy.
- Perhaps surprisingly the average deprecation of my Alfa Romeo cars per year has been lower at around 13.1%
- The average value of my personal cars, at £20,750 is very little different to the level of quality I expect from a company car, as these cost on average £20,400. You'll also be relieved to learn I'm sure that I look after company cars just as well as my own – they all get garaged every night and washed and polished with similar frequency. They also all get equally abused in terms of driving style or using them as work-horses to transport rubbish to the local refuse tip. Overall though I like my cars to always remain clean and tidy.

> **Editor's note** – I recall from your Aston Martin book that Mrs H doesn't say the same for your garage!
>
> **Author's note** – It's true, I do squeeze the car in amidst a lot of junk!

Hopefully then this helps you understand that as a car buyer I am relatively **traditional**, I don't naturally gravitate towards foreign cars nor do I buy and sell on a whim ( I know people who change cars every six months) or have little regard for the **financial consequences**.

These then are probably **not the traits you might obviously expect from anyone buying Alfa Romeo** – don't you need to be **brave** and foolhardy, or even an **Alfa Male?!**

**So how then did the final conversion to buyer take place?**

# Chapter 3

## The Test Drive & Shopping Around

I have already covered how Alfa now found itself with a rare place in my conscious mind and hence had at least earned a position on my prospective shopping list when I was ready to look for a new car. This then coincided with starting my own technology company so despite the added financial risk it seemed an appropriate time to go a bit up-market with my choice of car beyond say Rover and Vauxhall.

So I decided to shop for a new car by firstly evaluating and test-driving the following four brands only:

- **BMW** – I liked the saloons
- **Mercedes** – I liked the coupes
- **Jeep** – Unusual and a bit quirky
- **Alfa Romeo** – Peer pressure prompted investigation

My first port of call was **BMW**. We toddled off to the local showroom, liked the cars, sat in a couple, then took a seat to await a salesman. And waited, and waited and waited, so not exactly off to a great or courteous start. When we were eventually seen by a spotty young salesman he proceeded to tell us how everything was an extra cost option, the cars didn't even have a CD player or alloy wheels. On principle alone, we left.

Next step was **Mercedes**. The salesperson was a little older and more respectful but the overall experience was similar in many ways to BMW. Then when we started to discuss costs, (as at least a few extras **were** included in the base price for these nice cars), the subject of a discount for cash caused absolute **consternation** in the salesroom. The salesman genuinely looked shocked. He went off to ask the boss and came back with an offer of a **1% discount**. This derisory offer was another reason to leave quickly....not least because I had once achieved a 17% discount on a new Vauxhall!

> **Editor's note** – Wow, that's good.
>
> **Author's note** – Admittedly they did end up clawing a bit back once they'd realised they were selling at a loss but it turns out I was still getting a better discount than their staff member who delivered the cars!

We never then got as far as the **Jeep** garage (although these days that's often the same as the Alfa garage as both are part of the Fiat empire) so our **next trip was to Alfa Romeo**.

I pre-arranged an **Alfa Romeo** test drive by telephone and advised I wanted to come and test a Ti version, which I assume was a turbo, as this sounded more sporty. I think it was probably a **146Ti**, a mid-sized family saloon.

To my amazement, the sales guy said, and I quote, *"That's a pretty rubbish car. I'd be happy to take you out for an hour in the 146 but only if you ALSO go out for an extra hour in the new 156, which is so much better, in fact it's brilliant."*

My response was *"but I'm only interested in the Ti"* and he said, *"well you're not getting a go in one then!"* I kid you not, that's exactly what he said. Admittedly it was a different level of cheek to the BMW and Mercedes garages!

I was stunned in many ways. Not only was it a **surprise** response and a tad arrogant, it showed remarkable **honesty** and also **confidence** in the new Alfa. I was also surprised that compared to the can-hardly-be-bothered-to-see-you-approach at BMW and Mercedes, here was a salesman **willing to commit 2 hours of time and petrol**. I was sufficiently intrigued to **reluctantly agree** to go for the two test drives.

> **Editor's note** – I seem to recall the confidence was well founded. The Alfa 156 went on to win Car of the Year awards in several European countries?
>
> **Author's note** – Yes, I believe Alfa poached several key production staff from BMW so they could emulate the quality these brands achieve and it was probably a watershed moment for them and the start of the climb back to former glories of making **quality cars that worked**.

The day of the test drive at Alfa arrived, I turned up in my slow Freelander company car and went out for an hour in the 146Ti. It seemed a reasonable car which I would have been happy with, but was nothing to write home about. And then came the reluctant hour in the 156 which the salesman was forcing me into.

On this car it seemed to make most sense to test a 2 litre version (as I was previously used to a 200bhp fast Rover and wanted to use that as my benchmark re what a sporty car should be like) but again the salesman surprised me by saying *"the 1.8 litre is the better and more reliable engine" so we are trying that!"* And having learnt they weren't for budging, that's what we did!

It was a **really super test drive,** the salesman knew **everything** you could imagine about the car (whereas in the previous garages they generally seemed to know little detail if asked difficult questions, either about the brand generally or car specifically). He knew all about the specification, where it was built, the origin of the engine, designer, you name it.

It was a really **nice car to drive**, a great driving position, with everything **angled for the drivers convenience**, and it was quick and **superb around corners** which is something most former Mini drivers tend to crave. It also **sounded good** and had a superb **leather interior** on almost every available surface.

In fact the whole experience can be better summed up by James May, as you know of Top Gear fame....

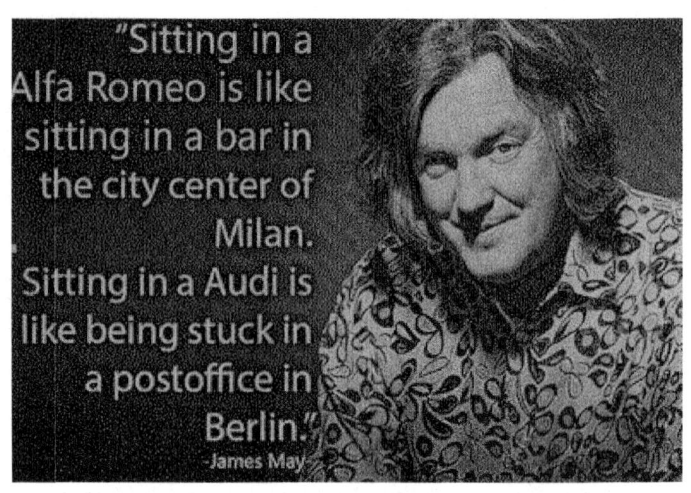

> "Sitting in a Alfa Romeo is like sitting in a bar in the city center of Milan. Sitting in a Audi is like being stuck in a postoffice in Berlin."
> -James May

NB. Apologies obviously to any Audi readers but as you'll know if you've read my books on Aston Martin, they're not exactly my favourite cars!

Back at the showroom we then sat down to discuss terms and I was astonished to discover how many

**extras were included** in the cost. In addition to things like a premium audio system and alarm the car had tinted windows, air conditioning, alloy wheels, a full leather interior.

In addition, the seating within the Alfa 156 together with the steering wheel and gear lever were upgraded and supplied by **Momo**, (The famous and sought after **Moretti-Monza** race-car accessory company). This alone would add £ thousands to a car like a BMW or Mercedes, not that the option exists, as it's even a cut above their own motorsport divisions accessories.

So I was more than a little surprised and impressed with the way the morning panned out. We even came close to concluding a deal on the very day of the test drive, but as I have said I like to be cautious and don't exactly rush into things.

> **Editor's note** – Yes, Mrs H says you make a major decision or change once every two years, that is: change car, move house, change jobs?
>
> **Author's note** – That's unfair. Only if I'm pushed!

## Back at home

After the test drive, and from the comfort of my armchair at home, I started researching alternative suppliers for a new Alfa 156, including the **Internet**, as this was just becoming a potential additional channel enabling direct-to-consumers for the manufacturers as we entered the New Millennium.

Anyway, it transpired that for whatever reason at Alfa Head Office (which presumably must ultimately mean Fiat?) they had got a bit worried about the emergence of the Internet and issued an edit to dealerships that they were to **beat any Internet price** revealed by a customer, so this netted me an **8% discount** off list price.

In addition, at the very point I was about to commit to my new car purchase, the exchange rate between the Euro and Pound dropped by about 10% making my pounds more valuable. So in a rare moment of good luck the cost of an Alfa, for a brief period plummeted as Italy had just switched onto the new currency.

Add all these factors together and I believe I got a deal on my 156 equivalent to around a 20% discount overall and around **35%-40% discount on a comparable specification German car**. Plus it wasn't really a comparable specification as I was also getting things like **MOMO** at no extra cost or hassle.

So having enjoyed the whole process of talking through the purchase with a super dealer, is it little wonder I dipped my first toe into the Alfa Romeo ownership waters and went ahead and confirmed by order with them?

> **Editor's note** – Sorry to go back a bit but I've never really understood why anyone would rave about one steering wheel or gear knob over another!
>
> **Author's note** – I was the same, until I drove a car with Momo accessories. They really do feel so **very different** in your hand that it makes driving a really **pleasurable** tactile experience and less of a chore.

In summary then, the test drive combined with an unusual dealer approach and a great deal got me my first Alfa Romeo. A **156 in red**, obviously, with a red leather interior, so it was a bit of a pimp mobile probably better suited to the streets of LA than sleepy Northamptonshire!

I have since been able to work out that I was acquiring an experience akin to owning a luxury car like an Aston Martin (minus a bit of speed and better sound-track) but for only about 20p in the £ of the latter brand.

Quite possibly I had stumbled on the **deal of the decade**, or had I? Would time and hassles or expenses prove me wrong?

The Alfa 156 – So cool it didn't even have rear door handles!

> **Editor's note** – And not bad for £15,600
>
> **Author's note** – This wasn't exactly like mine, it's the only black and white photo I liked!

# Chapter 4

## Not like other cars

Whilst we are waiting for my new car to be built and delivered it's as good a time as any to try and explain how in my experience buying an Alfa is a truly unique motoring experience, aside from the dealers that is!

So here are some fairly typical reasons that I have observed through all my cars:

<u>The design may not be logical</u> – for example, they made my Brera originally as a **design concept**. It was never intended to be a real car but they ended up making it after rave reviews at motoring trade shows around the world. As a consequence things like the shape of the boot are entirely **unpractical**, the suspension has had to be **over-engineered** to work (making it tough to replace), and the engine is a real squeeze, see below.

**Editor's note** – I see what you mean, not even room for a spare packet or matches!

Drivers matter – so Alfa tend to make everything **driver focussed** and not bother so much about passengers. So you can see the clock and speedo just fine, they probably can't! This doesn't mean they don't make the seats comfortable for front or rear passengers, they're super too but not the main focus.

It's Italian – so don't be surprised if it turns up with dials like the petrol gauge spelt in **Italian** as Benzina or the water temperature gauge as Aqua.

Because they can. The engineers often do stuff **just because** they can, they fancy having a go at a challenge, irrespective of whether conventional wisdom, say in a more sensible German car-plant, might be *'why bother'* or *'that will cost too much and lose us money.'* It's the same theory as to why the frame on the Shard and on my Gilera motorbike was visible (so the welds and construction had to be 100% perfect) whereas the sensible Japanese manufactures hid most of their welds and hence saved cost (on motorbikes – I don't know what the Japanese do on buildings and don't suppose they weld paper walls).

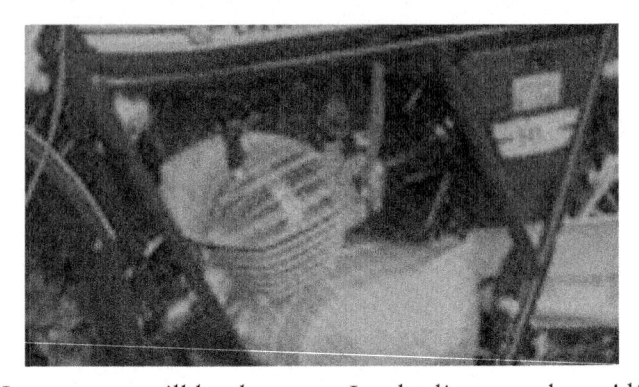

<u>No two cars will be the same</u>. I only discovered my Alfa Brera had 5 cylinders in its engine (and was 10 BHP more powerful than normal) years after I'd bought it when I was having a little bit of extra trouble getting parts, but I could still get them. **Who's ever heard of a 5 cylinder car** anyway? Especially when both the 4 cylinder and 6 cylinder versions are perfectly good. They probably just fancied seeing if they could squeeze it in! I've since heard that some Alfa Brera's have a glass sunroof but this is **hidden permanently** on the inside by a cloth headlining whereas mine has a powered 3 part hood on the inside!

> **Editor's note** – so that's NOT a sunroof or am I missing the point?
>
> **Author's note** – No, you're right. It looks like you have a sunroof on the outside but when you get into the car you haven't. some models don't have the headlining but neither do they have the powered cover! Go figure!

- **They buy job lots** – Alfa like working with some brands exclusively so as an example all my Alfas came with Pirelli tyres as standard, so far so good. But what's weird is that unlike with other cars whereby a particular size is always recommended and hence always fitted, this may **not be what you get** on your new Alfa. My only conclusion is that to make up for lost profits elsewhere when the engineers insist on mucking about (and probably partly out of the engineers inventive spirit of *lets just try it and see what happens,*) then Alfa can't resist taking whatever is Offer-of-the-Day from the favoured supplier.

- This might explain why you get cars with powered hoods and without them, or suddenly with things like a Momo steering wheel, or in my case, aerated leather seats (with tiny holes punched in – normally an expensive extra cost option) but free to me.

  **Editor's note** – This sounds like a generally good thing?

  **Author's note** – I think so, yes, I can't imagine they'd do anything detrimental to the driver, safety, or style. In the case of my Alfa 156 it created a most unusual and hugely enjoyable circumstance one winter. We live in a village with some steep hills and in winter even double-decker buses get stuck and only 4x4's can get through. But for some odd reason my 156 had very non-standard profile skinny tyres that cut through snow amazingly well. And in this particular year, even Range Rovers couldn't get through, but I still could in my low slung 156. Imagine their surprise at seeing a sleek saloon car sail by, at speed!

  **NB**. It wasn't so good with my next Alfa, a GT, this was atrocious in snow but superb in the wet, probably for similar reasons with an odd tyre choice!

Alfa GT

# Chapter 5

## Awaiting Delivery

At the turn of the millennium it was all the talk in business circles about Just-In-Time-Delivery making everything quicker and easier to produce. I was therefore pretty confident when ordering my new car that it would be with me in about **6-8 weeks,** at the outside, even though the dealer quoted about 3 months. So, not any different to other cars.

With the emergence of the Internet, buoyed up by Alfa managements obvious concern about it (hence the price matching) I was therefore eagerly expecting to be given a **precise time** slot as to when my car would be on the production line and I could obviously **watch it being made** remotely by video link. They hadn't promised this, I assumed.

> **Editor's note** – perhaps a tad optimistic?
>
> **Author's note** – That's me I'm afraid.

Anyway, you've guessed it, neither thing happened.

After a wait of a couple of months with **no communication** from the dealer other than confirmation paperwork, I chased up progress, expecting imminent good news. I was told *"expecting it in the next four months or so"*, I was obviously a little taken aback at which point the dealers thoughtfully added *"it's the annual local holiday in Naples, who knows when they'll decide to be back at work…. at least two weeks off for the whole factory is normal"*.

When I enquired about when it was booked into the factory, i.e. scheduled to be built, they said, "*You're funny, you've obviously never bought an Italian car before have you! Alfa don't work like that, we've just got to **cross our fingers** and **hope they do a batch of red cars soon**"*. Needless to say, nothing to watch on the Internet and the car came in about **six months** so even later than anticipated.

This long wait meant I **really appreciated** the car when it came – but it did add an extra pressure on getting rid of the old car. Luckily my old employer let me keep the company Freelander a bit longer.

# Chapter 6

## Snagging & First Impressions

When the car finally arrived and I picked it up from the dealers they were gracious enough to **apologise** for the delay, even though it wasn't their fault. They also were happy to commit almost an hour going through the fine detail of how everything worked – they didn't fob me off with just a bunch of flowers and the handbook.

In some respects that's a good thing – I discovered the radio manual is **written in Italian**. Upon questioning it I was advised *"what do you expect, it's an Italian car"*. After a bit of fuss it was agreed Head Office would order me an English version, albeit I was made to feel this was a special action on their part and I was the first person ever to complain!

- I have already mentioned how many of the dials etc have text in Italian too, these included the Rev counter, Petrol Gauge, and a few less obvious buttons, but strangely not everything. Some were in English and who knows if Italian Alfa drivers (in Italy) themselves also have to contend with some bits in English as that's just how things are!

We then started the long and arduous route of **breaking-in** a new car. Little **niggles** would occur and necessitate a trip back to the main dealer, they'd book the car in, supply a courtesy car and a couple of days later I'd pick it up again. Many of the faults weren't serious – things like rattles within trim in the back of the car.

As one thing was fixed, somehow they would manage to **break another piece** of trim that they'd had to remove to fix the first fault – I suspect as many parts of trim are push fit and not meant to be removed, severing lugs when you do.

So a fault that started, say, in the **boot**, gradually ended up moving towards the **front** of the car! In the end I asked them to just re-order a part that was rattling (now in the middle of the car) as I had **more confidence in my own ability to remove it carefully** and fit a new piece than the garage rushing and breaking something new. So that's how we solved things, using the good old postal system instead of Alfa mechanics at the dealership – but they weren't happy and I had to insist.

And once the snags were fixed I have had **almost zero defects on my various Alfas**, but more on that topic when we reach the relevant section of the book.

As I got to know the car and showed friends with more experience of engineering than me a few things became apparent:

- Alfa **don't always do things the obvious or easy way**. As I have intimated already then seem to do things "because that's the way an inventor or engineer / purist would, not an accountant"
- The engineering is **complex but robust** – why use one bolt if two would be better or safer seems to be a recurring theme.
- **Driver enjoyment** always comes first above passenger enjoyment or things like legroom and servicing simplicity.
- Options that others would charge for, Alfa often **include as standard**: "that's what a good driver needs"

- They are **heavy on tyres**. As cornering and holding the road well is an integral part of the Alfa experience wheels are often **aligned toe-in**. It works well but tyres don't wear evenly or last long.
- Engines are tuned for a **great drive** first, optimum speed second, so don't always expect to beat a GTi at the traffic lights! Fuel economy is often surprisingly good though.
- IMHO the **interiors** are crafted to the same great design and quality as the exterior, often with fine leathers – somewhat surprising as the car factories aren't generally in the midst of the Italian leather region. I guess that's simply another example of something Alfa feel a true driver deserves, whatever the cost. And I should add fancy coloured leather often costs no more than standard black.
- **Space** is for engineering. If there is a spare inch in the car, Alfa engineers will manage to **squeeze in** some gizmo or other in preference to things like luggage or passenger space!
- **Wind Tunnels are for planes.** Your Alfa will be made with first thought to its design and driving experience – so don't be surprised if the shape is a dirt magnet or rain runs into the boot or on your seat. Compromises to fix the latter won't be tolerated if they impact the former goals.
- **Forget Halfords.** It's not always easy buying After-Market accessories or even things like touch-up paint. With only around 5,000 cars a year being sold in the UK they're not usually on the list of compatible parts.
- Get any bits you need as part of the deal when you buy the car.
- I always make up the fact that any new car I buy has a small chip "*so why not send me some paint*

*rather than all the hassle of booking it in to the Bodyshop"* and they generally do.

# Chapter 7

## The Driving Experience

Right from the day when I took my first Alfa for a test drive to today, so that's almost twenty years later, I have enjoyed almost **every single day** I have driven my various Alfa Romeos, and a recent test drive in a 280 BHP Guilia confirms the latest models are just as good if not better.

In fact I would go further. Whist my Alfa's don't have the same engine sound-track as my Aston Martin, nor the same interior smell (as I love leather, but it's almost as good in an Alfa), nor quite the same fierce acceleration, I would say **I enjoy driving an Alfa more than an Aston costing 4-5 times more money**.

I think the Alfa is more **chuck-able** round corners, **feels safer, hugs the driver** better and instils more **confidence** overall. In short they are a **very refined drivers car**. Needless to say these aren't always traits favoured by passengers.

- To bring this concept to life a little I have driven my Brera round a 90 degree bend near home at 30mph (I was in a hurry) and managed to make the **tyre pop off the wheel**. The car continued completely safely, it didn't even alter the alignment or steering, just a slight change in road noise. I can't imagine this being possible in any other car.
  **Editor's note** – I noticed a caveat there. You said you loved the car almost every day?

**Author's note** – Good spot. My Alfa GT seemed to have a bit of an engine **flat spot**, so I paid about £150 for the CPU or something to be remapped to suit the UK climate better and it was transformed. Better acceleration, no flat spot, higher top speed and improved fuel economy. Money well spent.

Another feature that is very quickly discovered by Alfa owners is the sheer joy of finding a **winding road**. Not necessarily as curvy as the Stelvio Pass in the South Tyrol region of Italy, but any winding country road will do, and even better if you're particular model has seats that hug you and it happens to have good tyres for the job and weather at hand.

I have my own favourite winding road nearby which is a little nearer to home than Italy, Market Harborough in Leicestershire. It's perfect for a lovely and not too leisurely Sunday drive and luckily lies between our home and my mum's, between **Northampton and Leicester**. It's actually the B6047, a country road from just north of the market town (behind the McDonalds on a nearby roundabout), so you can grab a coffee before setting off towards Billesdon, to join the A47.

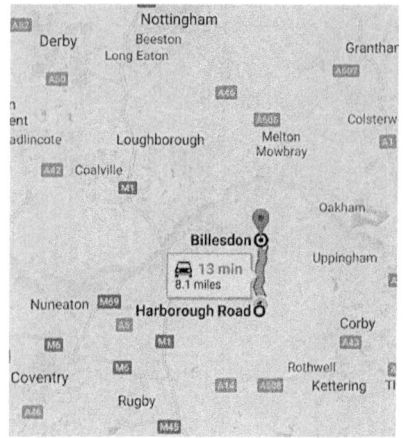

This is a popular route with motorbikes too and hence as you'd expect it's not the safest road in the county but it is one of the best to drive in any vehicle that enjoys corners and being glued to the road, so great in an Aston or an Alfa, particularly the latter where my confidence feels greater plus of course the potential for a huge bill is slightly less!

One important point to stress though is that given Astons unusual willingness to vary tyre choices during manufacture you can't take it as a given that the tyres on any Alfa, even a new one, are up to the job until you have a go, so **start off gentle and cautious** first!

>**Editor's note** – That certainly is unique advice!
>
>**Author's note** – Well I did say these are unique cars!

# Chapter 8.

## Pimp my Ride?

I have already alluded to the fact that you get **a lot for your money** with most Alfa models in terms of £ spent so I consider they offer great value, and unlike many cars that seem to lend themselves to being pimped up by owners (or the garages force expensive options on you), this hasn't been my experience with these cars. In short, the price you pay can often be the ticket price (less any discount for cash of course). With modern PCP deals Alfa are also often generous in throwing in rebates, low APR's and things like Free servicing, which can add up to a lot of savings over a longer ownership period.

The cars often have things like expensive large / wide alloy wheels as standard (and some of the nicest designs on the market) plus things like coloured brake callipers , flared wheel arches, stainless steel pedals and door guards, so there is really not a lot to be added even if you wanted to pimp your ride.

> **Editor's note** – I bet that doesn't stop you!
>
> **Author's note** – No. Whilst I've avoided the urge to add a go-faster strip or large numbers and a flag like on the General Lee, a Dodge Charger used by the Dukes of Hazzard, I have managed to find a few places to add decals to remind me who designed the car and what an unusual engine it has etc.

My favourite is the **Lusso** badge which I have added to what I think is called the rear quarter panel (behind the side rear windows) as whilst I love the style of the Brera from almost every angle, it is a bit chunky here – I think it's because said panel hides the rear passenger air-bags (I told you there are a lot of extras, this was 12 years ago!) and the design IMHO would have been improved with either chrome/brightwork window surrounds, or a badge. The later was a no brainer for about £10 and I sourced the badges online from Italy. I think it's an improvement anyway!

One other way I pimped my ride was to acquire a low-cost personalised number plate for £200 or thereabouts – this was mainly to mask the car age if I planned on keeping it for a decade if I could. The other benefit was being able to get as close as possible to the word Alfa or Brera, which as you can see, I did really well! It so obviously spells Alfa.

**Editor's note** – Perhaps you should have invested a bit more?

**Author's note** – A friend owns one of the world's leading Registration Plate businesses and he'd certainly agree, - he always makes jokes about my rubbish number plates. However, my dad had an expensive plate allegedly worth £10,000, we tried to sell it when he died, couldn't even shift it for £5,000. So you can see why I don't invest much!

PS. The number looks better in real life!

# Chapter 9

## The Garages

I think you will have gathered already that when it comes to buying a new car, you can't do much better than visit an Alfa Romeo showroom to enjoy a pleasurable sales experience. The sales people are generally really **interested in cars** and often know a great deal about the marque, this is something pretty unique, in fact it was **similar to visiting an Aston Martin showroom**, just a lot less expensive!

In almost every other garage I have ever visited, sales skills are the main interest area and it's not uncommon for the salespeople to **know almost nothing** about the actual cars they sell as they flit from brand to brand every few years working their way up the pecking order of brands. By contrast, Alfa sales people often stay for years content with lower salaries and you really can ask them almost anything. And as my experience has shown they will give **truthful** answers on most things – finance options possibly being the one exception as garages these days seem so heavily incentivised to hit finance numbers.

> **Editor's note** – Are you suggesting **car finance is not such a great deal?**
>
> **Author's note** – You could say that. Admittedly I haven't written a book about it yet!....but from some back-of-fag-packet calculations I have created in excel for my own use it suggests that a mixture of cash / personal loan (from a Bank or somewhere cheap like Zopa.com) could **save**

**£2,000 or circa 12% on the total** paid out eventually (versus PCP), and that's not even on a very expensive car. As we're not good here in the UK at spotting scams it's perhaps no surprise that **PCP is more popular in the UK** than any other country and we buy more new cars per head of population than almost anyone, even if we can't really afford them!

So that's sales, which includes when it's time to sell your Alfa, they are equally easy to deal with. But what about servicing and repairs?

I'm afraid this is probably the main thing that holds Alfa back as a brand. It's **not generally a great post-purchase experience**.

When it's time for a service of repair, sure the garages will be pleasant places with comfy seats, easy to book phone systems and free coffee. But in my experience it's the **work itself that suffers as it's generally done to a very poor standard**.

My conclusion is that as the number of Alfas on the road only represents about 0.2% of all cars, their simply aren't enough Alfas to create huge volume for training and experience purposes and nor is their enough cash floating around to pay top-dollar to staff. So the best mechanics and dealers probably, I assume, migrate to the top brands like BMW and Mercedes (the very best where the money is best, so that's Ferrari, Lamborghini, Bentley, Aston etc) and the lesser capable migrate towards Alfa, Subaru, Suzuki, MG etc. You get the idea.

I appreciate this is probably an unfair generalisation and there are bad staff in big brand dealerships and great staff in smaller dealerships, including Alfa

Romeo, but it's certainly been my experience and I have tried various different dealerships over the years.

This is **not to say that Alfa servicing and repair costs are inexpensive** – I have had £1,700 bills with my Alfa for a routine major service and cambelt which is on a par with the Aston Martin, I can only assume that's not the norm or the dealers don't make enough margin in other ways so servicing subsidises car sales etc?

This poor performance seems to translate into either jobs being **badly completed or tasks being delegated to unskilled trainees,** in either case you end up with a car that probably isn't fixed and will end up causing hassle. The good news: if anything major breaks as a result, you're **covered under the manufacturers warrantee.**

I tried various ways around the problem including changing main dealer for servicing (as you can go anywhere), this made no difference. I also tried **Independent Alfa specialists** – these were marginally cheaper but seemed if anything to be even more **routinely bad** at the job and with even less knowledge about the cars, which I never figured out. Maybe they too don't see enough to become expert?

I enjoyed **slightly better success with Independent All-Brand garages** that work on all makes of car, and mobile mechanics – I suppose these see every problem under the sun and in bigger volumes so generally have better all-round skills.

From a bodywork perspective I had just as high quality work, i.e. undetectable, using independent body repair shops as Alfa's own, and for a fraction of the cost, particularly if I paid a portion in cash!

> **Editor's note** – I can't imagine why!
>
> **Editor again!** – This all sounds a bit worrying – surely then it's almost impossible to own a

> trouble free Alfa as even if the car is well built, poor garages will ruin it and end up causing hassle for the owner?
>
> **Author's note** – This is true to a degree, but I did find a work around.

I discovered the best solution was to invest the time in **getting to know the one or two main mechanics in the Alfa dealership** by name, talk to them when booking the car in (not just the junior or dolly-bird on reception) and ensure they are keeping an eye on it personally, even if the work is delegated. This has great results, improved the quality and also on a few occasions enabled work to be part subsidized by the manufacturer even outside warrantee as they can make the case for you to Head Office and sign the necessary paperwork.

I also had an unexpected benefit – sometimes these mechanics also do **private work** – in one case I was able to keep my Alfa looked after by the top mechanic for probably a third of the dealer price, for years. Obviously this was after the warrantee had expired.

> **Editor's note** – Good point – are extended warrantees worth getting?
>
> **Author's note** – I only tried it once. It was such a palaver getting the car checked out first to ensure they'd accept it, I made one claim, they tried to wriggle out of most of the cost. So on balance I would say it's not worth while if you have a good Alfa and plan to look after it well in accord with the manufacturer's instructions as they are well built cars to start with and you can't get away with using a warrantee to fix a dodgy or poorly maintained car, as they will spot that.

# Chapter 10

## Problems Encountered

I really have had very few problems with any of my Alfa Romeos, and this is judged across an ownership period of nearly 20 years and three models.

Let's list out the issues minus teething problems fixed in the first few weeks under warrantee.

- **Key-Fob** – Needed a new battery after 2 years. **Cost £3**
- **Driver's Seats** – These seem to give up a bit around 80,000 miles, albeit the leather will still look almost like new. In one car, the 156, I hadn't realised but the mechanism to adjust the seat height had packed up so the new owner couldn't adjust it. But as I was the only driver, I never needed to alter it after I originally took delivery and got myself comfortable so genuinely had never noticed any issues. **Cost £Nil**

In my Brera, part of the lumbar padding and stitching had disintegrated so I could feel the metal frame through the leather at the base of my spine.

I resolved this by inserting a colour matched zip at the base and then I could easily add in a replacement piece of foam whenever needed at a later date. **Cost £7**, and it looks a lot better (like an invisible mend) in real life than it does here, honest!

Zipper Exposed (Never a good thing!)

In Use After Mending (Much better)

NB. The zip is almost completely hidden when the seat back is set back into a normal position, this has been photographed fully reclined so you can see what's hidden and what is possible on your own Alfa if you get one!

- **Driver's Window.** I have to use this a lot to access security gates at work plus on a Brera it automatically drops the window a fraction to open and close the door. So it all adds up to a lot of usage and it's no great surprise that this gave up closing

properly after about 8 years. The garage replaced the parts but couldn't get it to align correctly – and independent garage fixed it easily! Cost circa £230
- **Engine Flat-Spot.** As mentioned previously the Alfa GT had a flat spot when it lacked power. I fixed this by having a retune to give more power and better fuel economy but I would probably have tried this anyway for the power. Cost **£210/Nil**
- **EGR Valve** Exhaust Gas Recirculation system. This is a common and expensive problem on modern diesels as in an effort to make them more fuel efficient the technology that has been added to recirculate warm part used fuel just ends up sooting up the engine, in particular, the EGR valve gets bunged with particulates (pun intended). This is complex to fix and expensive. Luckily Alfa paid £2,000 under warrantee. Cost to me £225.
- My Brera now has this problem again but due to its age / residual value it is not IMHO worth a full repair and I have reduced the occurrence by using fuel additives. Cost £90
- I don't recall having any major MOT failures in 20 years, at least nothing that wasn't covered as part of a service / routine consumables like brakes, tyres etc.
- **Warning Light (**re Faulty Number Plate Bulb). This is probably my own fault as I have replaced a OEM bulb with a brighter long-life LED one. Cost £nil

- **Fog-Lamp (Broken Lens)**. Not really the fault of Alfa but the car got hit by a giant sheet of metal flying off a lorry on a motorway, at speed, which smashed into the lamp and not surprisingly popped it out of the car and broke the lens. It could have so easily been so much worse.

As I'm planning to sell the car soon I didn't want to splash out a fortune at the garage so researched whether I could just source a replacement glass and fit this with silicon. Turns out many parts for different Alfa models are standardised under the skin so you can often cut costs – I got two replacement lenses, albeit plastic from off a pair of aftermarket fog lamps for £10, so the repair was £5 and is mostly undetectable as you can see....I doubt if you can tell at a quick glance which is glass (original) and which is the newer plastic replacement....left or right?

(Answer = Left is the replacement)


If my maths are correct that's a total cost of about £770 on repairs over 19 years which works out at about the princely sum of just 11 pence per day! And it's less than 10 pence if I omit the tuning cost!

It's obviously hardly what people would expect when they call you brave for being an Alfa owner!

# Chapter 11

## Misnomers about Alfa Romeo

Obviously with any make of car you can get an unlucky Friday car (so-called as the employees were apparently keen to knock off for the weekend so rushed through production and often forgot key parts of the cars built on that day!) or just a bad one when the robot was having an off day. So with that proviso and using my own experiences of Alfa as a guide this is what I concluded the most common misnomers are:

**Rust Buckets?**

Perhaps the most common comment you'll hear from people who've never owned an Alfa. It was obviously a problem on cars from the **prior millennium** but in recent years I think it's fair to say the rust proofing is almost best in class as Alfa needed to put this reputation killer to bed and indeed they no longer score in lists of the top vehicles for rust. I have owned Alfa's up to 12 years old and the average age of all my models at sale was over 8 years old, and **not a one of them had any rust showing, anywhere**.

My current car, the Brera, being the oldest has literally just started (at 12 years) to have a small line of rust on the **inside** of one rear wheel arch (so not on the surface bodywork) and even that only took about 5 minutes with a bit of sandpaper and black hammerite paint to repair, and six months later and it hasn't worsened or even reappeared. So **rust is not generally a problem on modern Alfas** or even ten year old second hand ones and I have seen far worse on BMW's and most other makes.

### Breakdowns, Frequent?

This is probably the other main comment from non-owners. As the earlier section on my problems explained I have **not had any major issues with my Alfa Romeos in nearly 20 years**. And I can go one better than that, in all those years I have **never had a single roadside breakdown** or need to call out the AA or equivalent. And even when I've had a tyre problem the cars are so well balanced as to be able to **limp home** quite a few miles driving slowly despite only having three wheels – NB, I know that's not recommended but both front wheels were OK though and even the back wheels didn't get damaged without inflated tyres! So that's another myth I've not experienced.

### Constant Repairs?

Ditto I have **never needed to take my cars in for an emergency repair either**, anything that needed sorting could always wait until the car was in for a service, tyre change etc.

### Tinny?

I think this is a throwback to the cars from the 70-80's that had rust problems. This may have been due to inadequate painting and preservative or due to the use of thin metal, I don't know. What I can say is that when passengers get in and out of my various Alfas they have often commented on the **weight and substance** behind the doors – it seems unlikely then that metals are less thick than competitors. When you shut a door on an Alfa it does have a firm clunk to it as you would expect on a more expensive premium brand, I take that to be a good sign. So that's another myth busted.

## Badly built?

This is certainly the opposite to my experiences and indeed from mechanics I've used that work across multi-brands (rather than being tied to one marque) they have often commented how well built and solid the cars are, albeit sometimes they are put together in **quirky** ways as if the engineers rule the roost at Alfa, not designers or accountants. And I think that's a fair criticism and part of the cars charm. If anything, as I have alluded too already they may even be **over-engineered** in places, but surely that's a generally good thing, especially in areas like safety. No one ever complains that Volvo have a solid reputation in this area.

## Shoddy Parts / Plastics?

This is probably a subjective comment as the kind of plastics that one driver or passenger likes, another may not. With many manufacturers upping their game in this area in recent years I would say that Alfa are built with an **appropriate quality** – it wasn't any better or worse than my Aston Martin albeit it may not be best in class like a Bentley or Audi say. But I have never had any parts break so don't think the accusation of being shoddy has any merit on newer cars. And having recently test-driven a Lexus I would consider the plastics used are **higher quality** on the Alfa Romeo.

## Expensive?

Again this may be relative depending on what other cars people are considering. On a personal level I have always found that Alfas offer extremely good value given the specification of engines and extras that are generally included in the price. And they offer even better value if you buy second-hand with part of the original warrantee in place or do a great used deal / trade-in.

NB. A friend has recently leased a top of the range **Kia** Stinger GT (244BHP). It's a lovely car with loads of gizmos and actually is on paper about 10% cheaper than a similar specification Alfa Guilia Lusso. But the story doesn't end there – with discounts you could **buy either car for the same approximate cash price** of about £33,000. The **Alfa though has 15% more power, 20% better MPG, and faster acceleration**, so surely it's the better deal and not so expensive after all? If you then factor in that the Alfa also gets slightly **better user reviews**, has elements of **Ferrari technology** in its DNA, has a perfect **50%/50% weight distribution** AND is **ten groups lower to insure** then I know which I'd chose!

## Depreciation

This is of course also a factor in cost but I have more conclusions on that later – it deserves its own section of the book!

> **Editor's note** – Bet we all can't wait for all those figures!

> **Author's note** – I promise it's not as detailed as some of my other books!

## Prohibitive Insurance.

See the comment above regarding an Alfa being 10 placings lower in the insurance tables than a similar specification Kia. In addition it's often even cheaper if you buy insurance through the Owners Club, irrespective of whether you bother to go to any meetings or not. I don't bother with this and my insurance for the 210 BHP Brera 5V Turbo is **still** only about £350 per year, and that's including full AA cover. So unless you have a bad driving record or are very young, insurance doesn't seem to be an issue on even the better specification models.

## Cambelts & Clutches

I believe there is a misconception that these either always go wrong or wear out very quickly. I have **never had a single clutch replaced in over 240,000 miles** of Alfa motoring and provided you keep up with your regular servicing intervals (with a reputable mechanic) I have no reason to suspect any issues with the cambelt either – In fact I may have missed one of these services on the Brera and at 97,000 miles it's still going strong.

### Dodgy Electrics

I think with any modern car there is a tendency for electrical problems to become more of an issue as more and more technology is added to cars each year. Traditionally Italian products (such as motorbikes) had a bad reputation in this area as nothing was well shielded from the wet which may not matter in Milan but it certainly matters in Manchester. Aside from the rear number plate warning light on my Brera and a key-fob battery on the 156 I have had **no issues** like this. My final word on the subject of electrics is *watch out for new cars with missing rear lights – 10 to 1 they will be French cars not Italian ones, not even Fiats!*

### You're Brave!

In summary then, do you need to be brave and perhaps foolhardy to own an Alfa Romeo? I certainly think that case is **well and truly busted**, especially if it's one of the more modern models since the new millennium. For my Brera only around 2% of the cars sold in the UK are taken off the road each year, so even with only 2,400 or so left, they may still **hang around for another 50 years** at least – this is pretty good given that in the main these will be high performance cars. I can't think of many marques where cars can be expected to survive just a 15 year life span before they meet a crusher in a scrap yard, but Alfa do seem to have better longevity.

# Chapter 12.

## The Truisms

OK, I've hopefully dispelled some of the popular misconceptions about Alfa Romeo, or at least as far as I can through my own limited experience of three model ownership since the new millennium. But what about the things you may have heard that are true about this unique brand?

### Great Design

It doesn't apply to every model of course (personally I think the Guiletta is a bit of a stinker) but generally it's fair to say that many Alfas have stunning design, particularly externally, usually undertaken with the assistance of **Pininfarina or Giugiaro** Design Studios. And as I have already mentioned the interiors can be great in leather plus every aspect of the cars is made to be *just-right* for the driver.

I seem to recall also that in the past an Alfa was selected as the **only car ever to be allowed into a museum as a permanent example of excellence in product design** – but look as I may I can't find it so it must have been somewhere with nothing to do with cars in the normal course of events.

### History

Lots of cars have history going back a century but not many have survived and those that have typically lose their once famous innovative edge. Alfa are a bit different, they still come out with products that make little sense in a world of industrial design and ergonomics, **they make it because they just want to** and I applaud them for that.

Plus of course not many brands can lay claim to having Mr Ferrari drive for them or winning the first Grand Prix – and it's nice to see Alfas making a bit of a comeback in this area in recent years.

## One Big Club

Whilst the days of fellow owners **waving** at each other in the manner of which AA mechanics used to salute to members driving past is of course a thing of the past but with so few Alfas on the road (circa 100,000 out of about 35,000,000 million cars in the UK) it's not that unusual to still be acknowledged by owners of the same model of car. It might just be a brief flash of the lights or letting you out at a junction but it's still nice and relatively rare with other cars in a fast paced world where no one has time for each other anymore.

And the owners' clubs are very friendly and worth visiting as a guest just to size them up. Owners are also very helpful on the various online forums so if you do get a problem or have a difficult to resolve question, someone in the world will usually offer good advice or point you in the direction of a useful supplier.

## Quirky

If you are looking for a vehicle where everything makes sense, is practical and has been researched within an inch of its life I would suggest buying German, not Italian. If you like the idea of a car that has everything it should have, and maybe even a few extras, but they are **not necessarily in the places you'd expect them, buy an Alfa.** As an example, my Brera has handy hooks in the boot to hold luggage safe, but can you reach them without dirtying your clothes, of course not! And things like the button to open the boot or plug in a OBD signal sender will be hidden somewhere you can't get to easily!

On this point I have to say it's nice though sometimes to own something that feels like it was designed and built by man (or woman) and not a machine or computer program. You get that rare feeling with Alfa Romeo.

> NB. I remember a car salesman a few years back shocking me with a tale about how a new Ferrari they had just taken delivery of straight from the factory immediately needed to go into a body-shop to have some paintwork blemishes fixed and panels realigned as the gaps between panels weren't consistent. My Aston was a bit like this too as they are in-part handmade.

It's not quite as bad as this with an Alfa but I doubt if the panels fit quite as precisely as they will on the Kia or a German or Japanese car! Maybe Alfa engineers even set the robots up intentionally to make things a bit **varied** as that's more interesting!

# Chapter 13

## Living with Alfa Romeo

This is certainly not a case of unlucky 13, at least not in my 19 years' experience.

If having an Alfa was a pain in the proverbial I certainly wouldn't have owned these cars continuously for this length of time and now be considering my next new one. It's fair to say that I consider Alfa Romeo to be very easy to live with and despite the reputational issues they have caused less hassle than my Rovers, Land Rovers and Vauxhalls.

That said, there are some caveats to be considered for prospective owners as follows:

### DIY...Not!

I'm not suggesting for a minute that these are cars you should attempt to look after yourself, I think they are generally too complex for that. But it is healthy to have an approach towards being willing to research things about the cars yourself, for example, on user forums online, so if you do decide to venture out beyond the main dealer network, you can give some useful tips to your mechanic. As an example, I discovered late in the day that my car is a relativity rare 5 cylinder engine, I assumed it was 4, so some consumables are a little harder to source or fit differently. They may not have spotted this immediately themselves.

> **Editor's note** – I'm surprised, no amazed, that you dint know what you were buying!

> **Author's note** – As Mrs H can testify, I am generally fairly laid back and even though I love my cars, I'm not such a geek as to know every little detail about them. My car was a colour combo I was after, the right age, mileage, price and engine size. So that was what mattered, not the number of cylinders. It was a small bonus when I discovered, for sure!

The dealers aren't the most helpful in the world (in the service departments) and **forget getting any help from Alfa Head Office themselves**. I have asked them questions on several occasions and have **never** had the courtesy of even a reply, never mind a proper answer. Even Aston Martin are better than that, they reply eventually!

> NB. I must digress for a moment and **commend Vauxhall** on this point. Many years ago I had a Vauxhall cavalier which started bubbling oil up through the carburettor and back out through the air filter and out onto the road through the air intake – something that was literally unheard off. The main dealer couldn't solve it in a couple of weeks so they contacted Vauxhall Head Office who had their technicians on the case, literally on-site. In the end they removed the whole engine, took it apart, drilled extra oil breather holes into the engine casing, reassembled and got it working without a fault. When I heard all this I expected an invoice larger than the value of the car but I had a pleasant surprise, the only charge was about £4 for a new gasket. When I queried this they said it was good experience for all the top mechanics and engineers at the Dealership and Head

> Office so they were happy to pick up the cost even though the car was out of warrantee.

I wouldn't count on this from Alfa although they have on occasion **contributed** to costs if the mechanics stressed things had worn away too quickly.

> **Editor's note** – I see now why you said earlier it's good to build a rapport with the mechanics.
>
> **Author's note** – Yes, especially if they also run their own garage on the side. In the case of my tame mechanic, his side-line business also had an almost identical name to the main dealer – I won't quote the real names here but let's say one was called Alfa Midlands, he picked Midlands Alfa for his smaller garage. Then when he stamped the service book at first glance it looked as if you had continuous service at the main dealer, especially if he forgot which stamp to use if I dropped the car off in his lunch break at the real garage!

### Regular Servicing

I know I have already talked about this but I think it's a drum worth beating again. As these are complex vehicles it's **important not to skimp on servicing** by forgetting, letting service intervals lapse, or using cheaper parts. So as an example I always use the **best low friction oils** and as I have said find a good mechanic who uses genuine parts.

> **Editor's note** – hang on, you've admitted that your Brera may have missed a vital cambelt change?
>
> **Author's note** – well spotted, that's true. However I have had my latest mechanic (as a previous one has retired) check out the cambelt for wear and there is none evident. If the car

were a petrol model I would probably be keeping it off the road for posterity as a future classic car but as it's a diesel (which the government seems intent generally to drive off the roads), 12 years old, and has almost done 100,000 miles I now regard it as basically at the end of its useful life. So I'm minimising expenditure to save towards a replacement, in short, I'm taking a chance that the mechanic is correct and it's either been replaced (but forgotten) or isn't needed, but I wouldn't normally do this, especially on a newer more expensive car. It's a shame really as the Brera is a super car, it is in near perfect condition inside and drives as nicely as the day I got it.

## Tyres, and lack of

I have already mentioned that these are prone to wear quicker than expected due to many Alfas being set up as toe-in (so the tyres aren't sitting square /face-on to the road). Some garages insist on correcting this when they check the **tracking** (incorrectly, and make assumptions rather than follow the manufacturer settings) but when they do this the cars don't drive anything like the same so IMHO it's best to stick to what the manufacturer Alfa Romeo recommended as new.

However the practicalities of this are that you need to remember to turn the front wheels to full lock occasionally when parking so you can properly **check out the inside hidden tread** of the front tyres especially. On more than one occasion I have discovered much to my horror that I have tyres with **lots** of spare tread on the outside but they are **worn down to the wire innards** (the strengthening inner layer sandwiched between wafers of rubber, i.e. the radial of the tyre) on the **inside** treads, which is obviously very dangerous but easily missed.

For this reason I **always pay extra for my tyres and fit almost top of the range** such as Pirelli P Zero tyres with amongst the highest speed rating and so far they have not let me down. The downside of course is that these are almost 300% of the cost of cheaper brands like Nagkang or Toyo.

# Chapter 14

## Running Costs

I haven't collated all my Alfa costs over a 20 year period as that would be a bit weird but what I have got is a complete breakdown of almost a decades full cost comparison with my Aston Martin versus the Alfa Brera, and this runs till about six months ago when I sold the former. I think it makes for surprising reading.

The Aston Martin was mostly used on a daily commute or for journeys under 5 miles, whereas with fuel economy 300% higher, the diesel Alfa was used for longer journeys or when I was travelling to places that were less salubrious or may have had uncertain parking.

> **Editor's note** – uncertain parking?...do you mean you weren't certain if you'd want to park or could find a space?
>
> **Author's note** – Neither! I mean that I didn't know the parking situation well and wouldn't have wanted to go in the more expensive car only to find it was a tight squeeze so I'd end up with a ding in the door, or maybe the kerbstones were narrow, so I'd knock a chunk out of the alloys. I still wouldn't have wanted to park even a 12 year old Alfa anywhere it could be vandalised or stolen.

On that note, when I was between proper cars with the low cost Austin Mini that I sold for a profit, I went out one night in it for a company treasure hunt, parked my car by the roadside in a reasonably lit area that was part residential, part industrial, I then went off in someone else's car for the hunt only to come back and find that all the Mini windows except the windscreen had been smashed. And it was the first day of my insurance.

> **Editor's note** – you must have been upset and well out of pocket?
>
> **Author's note** – I wasn't out of pocket as the insurers were great and it turns out they **really don't care even if you claimed 1 minute into the insurance** as "somebody always has to be first" and "that's what insurance is for". But what upset me the most was the villains didn't steal my music collection – which must say something about my taste!

It just goes to show that you can't be too careful when parking.

Anyway, enough about that, you'll want to know about the running costs? Here is a summary:

|  |  | Aston Martin V8 Vantage | Alfa Romeo BreraS 2.4 Diesel |
|---|---|---|---|
| First Aquired |  | 12th Jan 2012 | 1st Nov 2010 |
| Sold |  | 15th Oct 2018 | Still Owned |
| Mileage Covered |  | 19,775 | 59,193 |
|  |  |  |  |
| Depreciation | ❶ | £ 13,000 | £ 11,750 ❶ |
| Service / MOT / Repairs | ❷ | £ 7,985 | £ 4,550 ❸ |
| Fuel (Estimate) | ❸ | £ 7,740 | £ 10,304 ❷ |
| Insurance / Breakdown |  | £ 3,250 | £ 3,125 |
| Road Tax |  | £ 2,015 | £ 1,790 |
| Tyres |  | £ 965 | £ 1,540 |
| Insurances Excess re Claims |  | £ 250 | £ - |
|  |  |  |  |
| Cost Per Annum |  | £ 5,216 | £ 4,076 |
| **Total Monthly Cost** |  | **£ 435** | **£ 340** |
| **Total Cost Per Mile** |  | **£ 1.78** | **£ 0.56** |

As you can see the **Alfa Brera** has cost around £30,000 to own, tax, fuel, service and insure over an 8 year period which equates to about **£340 a month**, including vat. With almost 60,000 miles being covered in that car, so almost 8,000 per annum, the **rate per mile is £0.56** which of course, as expected, makes a mockery of the seemingly generous £0.45 per mile which HMRC allow for company mileage claims – in short, you can't even claim the real running costs of your car back and if you use your private car for work you are potentially subsidising your company by over 10 pence per mile. The reality for many people will be worse than this as I believe I have kept my Alfa costs to an absolute minimum due to things like seeking cheaper mechanics.

> **Editor's note** – Mrs H also tells me you have been known to freewheel in neutral down hills to save petrol?!
>
> **Author's note** – I'm afraid that's true although obviously I don't switch the engine off as that is dangerous when the steering suddenly locks on a bend! As to whether it saves petrol is a matter of much debate with my more technically minded friends – they say not (as the car knows it's not under any pressure to supply power so cuts the fuel being emitted by the fuel injection, totally) I say I don't think it cuts it as fully as my depressing the clutch so all it needs is a small bit of fuel to idle. I've now researched it more thoroughly for the book and it looks as if I was wrong and have been wasting fuel for years! So my Alfa Brera's already credible **35mpg average** MPG could even have hit 40 if I'd known what I was doing!

https://www.team-bhp.com/forum/technical-stuff/102829-does-coasting-save-fuel.html

The comparison with the **Aston Martin** which has an engine twice the size and is naturally aspirated without a turbo or supercharger is perhaps to be expected, despite the much lower 2,500 miles per annum that car averaged out at **£1.78 a mile**. Still, as I always said, *if you can afford the car, you can afford the fuel, quit moaning and offset some carbon*, so I did.

> **Editor's note** – Sorry, you've offset your carbon? How?
>
> **Author's note** – Obviously I set up a carbon offset scheme just for us! We've used it for all the company employees to offset all the carbon used in journeys to work and for private motoring, plus the energy used by the company – and we've achieved it by investing in wind and solar energy farms.
>
> **Editor's note** – Why am I not surprised!

The other interesting things to me within this data are that even if you buy your cars very prudently, as I like to think I do, **depreciation is still the number one cost overall.**

Again in researching for this book I have discovered that the new electric cars are by far the fastest depreciating on the market, (although that is allegedly changing slowly now) and with the possible exception of Tesla (and to a lesser degree top end BMW's and Lexus due to the luxury aspects) you could fork out £30,000 on a very small basic EV only to find it has lost £25,000 in value in just 3 years, that's **£700 a month** depreciation and more than the total running costs for even my Aston Martin!

**Fuel costs are of course generally the next largest cost** when running a car hence the importance for both the environment and your pocket of getting a car that returns a good MPG figure – and in the main I would say Alfas are amongst the best at this which I guess is only to be expected when they can borrow know-how from sister companies such as Ferrari with their F1 pedigree.

> NB. I have already commented earlier how a similar specification Kia at the same price offers 20% worse MPG and 15% less power, so **Alfa are good at getting a quart out of a pint pot** (although they needed a bit of help with my Alfa GT). They may not be best on class as more fuel efficient cars will of course exist but I would be surprised if they offered anything like the combined efficiency and overall value, fun and style as an Alfa.

The **tax** costs for the Alfa are of course quite high as gradually the government are trying to price diesel cars off the road, and the insurance comparison versus the Aston is skewed slightly as the Aston was particularly good value as I opted to have an annual mileage limit in place and couldn't drive more than 250 miles per month. No such limit existed on the Alfa and this car could also be used for Business, which carries an extra premium.

**Servicing, MOT's** and the odd repair were the next highest costs after depreciation and fuel at around £500 a year but as this included consumables such as brake pads, disks and top of the range oil and plugs I don't think these costs are excessive at all for the Alfa Romeo and are around what you would pay on most lease deals per month if you opted for a "with maintenance" deal, and that's with them being able to negotiate trade deals in bulk.

In summary then I would say that an **Alfa like my Brera can be a reasonably economical car** to run, and this is particularly true if you keep it for longer so the depreciation rate flattens out over time, aided by achieving savings on main dealer costs where possible.

# Chapter 15

## Depreciation.

As this seems to be the largest cost for any driver and also because it was one of the oft-heard rumours about Alfa Romeo that they suffer terrible depreciation in value from new, I thought this merits a section all of its own.

My conclusions are as follows:

- As I generally keep my Alfa's for quite a few years my **average depreciation per annum is 13.1%.** In most cases it's **actually around 10%** per annum (but is skewed by the 18% rate for my Alfa GT which I sold very quickly as I wasn't happy with fabric seats constantly getting wet in the rain!)
- By comparison to all the other cars I've owned the average rate is 15.1% per annum but rises to **16.8% per annum** if I exclude the very slow depreciating Aston Martin Vantage. NB. This excludes the Mini owned for 6 months on which I made a small profit as this excludes hundreds of pounds of labour to smarten up the car for sale!
- So overall it's probably·fair to compare an average of 13.1% for Alfa and 15.1% for the rest, suggesting that if you own these cars for a decent period of time (my average being 6 years) then **depreciation on an Alfa could be 15% less than normal costs** – it's certainly not any worse, which was good to see in hard numbers as it confirmed my suspicions. Obviously if you purchase at full book price and sell badly or quickly you can expect high

depreciation, as you will for most cars other than supercars or German brands which seem to hold value best of all.
- Looking at my higher end Alfas such as the Brera I paid £13,500 for a 3 year old car which was around £27,000 new, so it had already lost 50% of its value in the first 3 years with a previous owner. **This is the same rate of loss that the trade anticipate for the top of the range new Guilia Quadrifoglio.**

> **Editor's note** – That's good to see that your comparison should still hold water today, but tell me why did the GT do so much worse?
>
> **Author's note** – As I've said **I sold that car in a hurry and hence lost 25% in just 18 months**, so I suppose this was all the dealers mark-up to be covered in just a year, which is a big ask. And this was despite it being a nice Limited Edition model in good condition so there must be a clear lesson here, don't buy these cars on a whim if you're not exactly sure it's the model you want. I learnt from this and took an age to find the right Brera.

Back to the depreciation plot.

For the book I have completed some more detailed analysis of Alfa Depreciation and it's interesting to note that in one of the most comprehensive surveys completed in 2016 by Cap-HPI there **is no single Alfa in the top 25 list of high depreciating cars**.

> NB. Even some less reputable surveys didn't really have much to show the truth of the Alfa depreciation enigma although one suggested the new Alfa Guilia, despite being a great car with a 4+* user / motoring journalist rating, might

**creep in at position 10,** but it's still not that bad, well I don't think so!

# Chapter 16

## Selling the Wheels.

Selling an Alfa is always an interesting experience – they are relatively easy to sell online, or at least get trialists along for a test drive, as the cars have a sporty reputation. Getting people to part with sensible amounts of cash is a little harder though, due I am sure to the aforementioned **misnomers** which make people cautious about ongoing expected costs for repairs.

> NB. When buying second hand it is certainly essential to ensure the car has a **solid pedigree** in terms of service history with routine work all carried out on time.

Because I tend to specify nice interiors for my cars I generally don't have a problem selling them on as people often ask me to let them know **privately** when my car is coming onto the market, often years in advance. This happened to my first Alfa, the 156, which went to a family friend. I was 100% happy with said car and only changed it for a new Alfa as I'd been tempted by a GT and the 156 was getting a bit long in the tooth – it came as something of a shock when after the event they alerted me to faults on the driver's seat (mentioned earlier) which I'd never noticed. Despite this I could probably have sold the car for more, further reducing the depreciation figures. I also had an offer like this for the GT but couldn't take advantage of it as when the right specification Brera came along, I had to move quickly!

The GT wasn't really a sensible purchase as I like my leather interiors (this is a throwback to a family working in the shoe trade and I had many happy an hour playing in the leather warehouse so got the smell of leather into my DNA). I had decided to change said car almost immediately after buying it but it took a while to find a Brera with just the correct specification, so when this appeared on the scene I had to move fast. This meant a trade-in was the best option, albeit an expensive way of selling a car as you don't get the best price. Luckily this hasn't mattered too much as I've loved the Brera so much that I've kept it even longer than the data in this book suggests so it's achieved the lowest depreciation rate of all my Alfa's anyway, despite paying over the odds at trade-in time.

As I am planning on changing the Brera this year (and can take my time whilst I wait for a new car to be built), I have started (six months ago) to explore new options with regards to parting with the Brera, starting with the trade.

- My first port of call was a **Vauxhall** dealership – somewhat surprisingly I went for a test drive in a very smart Insignia (which had one of the most luxurious leather interiors I've seen on a car recently). I didn't really want a trade in price but the dealer insisted, and as the car had just been polished it was as good an idea to benchmark the cost as at any other time.
- So they did a full mechanical check up on a ramp, went for a test drive, pronounced it in **perfect mechanical order** (something which surprised them for a 12 year old car) and offered me **£1,750 cash**, whether I bought the Vauxhall or not.

I then thought I'd check this against one of the **online buying websites,** as you can see from my screen grab from my mobile (complete with Aston screen saver) the offer was marginally better at £1,805 although these guys haven't seen the car and may negotiate down later?

> 15:45  .ull 4G

20 October
18:12

All Photos

18:12

Saturday 20 October

**MESSAGES**  25m ago

**TrustedCarB**
You can sell your car today A7FVA for £1,805.00 to book an appointment now click here > https://tx.v

The next port of call is obviously to check how much these cars sell for either privately or through dealerships and the best place to check that (based on sheer volume of stock) has to be **Autotrader.**

This is the nearest specification model I found – it's even the V5 engine version with a sun-roof so all that's varying from my model is that it's a year older registration.

With **every year of ownership generally losing 10%** of a vehicle's value but **with each 1,000 miles** driven either **adding or losing 1% value,** I think it's fair to conclude at best my car is worth 10% more than this if advertised privately – so let's settle for an **estimated value of £4,950** which might equate to as much as £6,750 if it was sold on via a garage with a limited warrantee provided to the new owner.

So what's the conclusion?

Obviously if the car is without faults it makes sense to **aim for a private sale,** maybe settling at something like £4,250 which is **still £2,500 more (almost 60%) than the garage offered**. In my case with the intermittent EGR valve issue needing looking at I really need to trade in.

# Chapter 17

## Owner Loyalty

The fact that you are reading this book probably suggests that you are already well aware that Alfa Romeos, almost unique amongst car brands, seem to have a legendry audience of passionate followers. Given the also legendry misnomers about problems, is it true or all a myth?

I've attempted to work this out from published data and this is what I've concluded:

- According to Mixpanel's 2017 Product Benchmarks report, for most industries, the **average customer retention rate was below 20%**. In the media or finance industries, retention over 25% is considered above average. This all seems reasonable and matches some of my own observations managing Marketing campaigns for clients in various industries. But what about car ownership?

**AutoTrader** estimate that on average in the **UK 57% of car buyers change brands each time they change their car,** so loyalty (at 43%) for cars is almost twice as good overall as for products and services in general.

If we assume most cars typically stay on the roads for around a decade, there are only circa **91,000 Alfa Romeos on UK roads** (from recent Government statistics), which **suggests a much higher set of loyalty percentages for Alfa**, which means **either loyalty is a lot higher or these cars are so well built that they last <u>much</u> longer** than ten years – either scenario is good for the argument that they are in fact **great cars!**

Sticking to the 10 year figure combined with statistics about the number of Alfas sold here each year and, assuming my mathematics are correct (and I'm not bad at maths, scoring 99% in my school final exams) then I arrive at a **potential retention rate for Alfa Romeo of 54% per annum, so almost a quarter better than cars generally**. Hardly what you'd expect with a brand with such a historically negative reputation, or at least amongst non-buyers.

In addition to this strong story, consider that I'm **about to buy my fourth Alfa in a row – there is only circa a 8% chance of a typical car buyer being in the same brand after 4 cars**, and if the 20% loyalty noted in most industries were to apply to cars (and Autotrader are wrong) then these **odds fall to just 1% chance.** So only one buyer in a hundred would be in the same car after selling three times, this plainly **makes me quite unusual!**

In actual fact with only 4,100 Alfas being sold in the UK (across all models) in the UK now each year, after four changes the chances of a buyer still being in an Alfa (at the standard 20% product loyalty rate) is actual **Nil, which in theory makes me unique!**

But again, if I use my maths as the base **the truth could be that there is actually a UK Alfa Romeo driver out there who loves the brand so much that he or she is actually on their 15$^{th}$ car from Alfa** (This is assuming the above sales rates and 57% loyalty)

I have no proof of this but one statistic which surely points us in the direction that loyalty really is high and multiple repeat buyers do exist is the fact that 3,000 people belong to the Alfa owners club – and that's with only 4,100 being sold each year, most of whom probably don't join.

My conclusion then about Alfa Romeo loyalty is that it's so good I'm only surprised that the bright-sparks (not twin-sparks) at Alfa haven't introduced some kind of Lifetime Ownership Package for buyers – simply agree to keep paying a monthly fee forever and in return keep getting a new Alfa model every few years. I'd sign up.

> **Editor's note** – Twin Spark?
>
> **Author's note** – It's an Alfa joke! The engines have twin spark engines so it increases power and fuel burning efficiency.

This is what Wikipedia has to say....

> **Alfa Romeo Twin Spark (TS)** technology was used for the first time in the Alfa Romeo Grand Prix car in 1914. In the early 1960s it was used in their race cars (GTA, TZ) to enable it to achieve a higher power output from its engines and in the early and middle 1980s, Alfa Romeo incorporated this technology into their road cars to enhance their performance and to comply with stricter emission controls.

# Chapter 18

## Whatever next?

Picking my next car is obviously a little difficult as having just sold my Aston Martin (the subject of another Bite-Sized Book, as that wasn't easy either!) it's going to be very hard to be satisfied. Almost whichever car I pick will probably be less luxurious or less stylish or less powerful, unless of course I want to splash out £200,000, which I wouldn't, even if I could.

Then there is the question to be answered as to which car suits best as not just an experience or set of features, but which is the brand I feel **matches my own personality** best?

- As you can already see I am a big advocate of Alfa Romeo and I cannot really express in print how much I was looking forward to their replacement for cars like the 159 and GT a few years ago, this was when they launched the Guiletta to much fanfare.
- We were even privileged enough to be invited to the manufacturers launch at the Exhibition Centre in Birmingham so eagerly took a day off work to travel over, see the range, and hopefully order a new one. But what a let-down – the car seemed to be uninspiring from the outside – a mish-mash of styles, and ugly on the inside. In part because the early models had few refinements like nice leather interiors.

So deciding to stick with this brand isn't always easy, but luckily it feels as if **now is a good time to buy Alfa** as they are back on form with some good looking cars again, and these are capable of again winning Car of the Year awards and getting onto the Top Gear Cool Wall for sure.

So I have almost certainly made up my mind that only an Alfa or possibly a Maserati (if the price is right on a nearly new model) meets these odd mix of needs. These brands offer me the right balance of quirkiness, performance, value and are sufficiently unusual as to not feel as if I am simply following the crowd.

Due to practicality, this is pointing in the direction of four Alfa models and I am interested in:

- The **Guilia 280 bhp petrol saloon** – available from between £34,000-£41,000, I'd probably go for a red or tan leather interior. Due to advances in technology and turbo this is better performance than my Brera and when pushed didn't feel to be losing much ground to the Aston, so it would be a good middle ground and I think it's a great looking car. It was great on a test drive and lots of extras are included in the price, as usual.
- The **500+ bhp Giulia Quadrifoglio petrol saloon** – for circa £60,000 for one of the fastest cars on UK roads, in fact I think this is more like a road-going F1 car . If I could get this with a bespoke full leather interior I would jump at the chance but as they are supplied with a standard interior which is mostly black, I am unlikely to proceed down this route.
- The **Stelvio 4x4 280 bhp SUV** at about £47,000. Just as nice as the saloon but around £6,000 more expensive to be a bit higher off the ground. Hence the consideration of a one-year old Maserati Levante instead which feels a little bit more like a bespoke SUV designed for the purpose than a saloon car on stilts.

- Or the **Stelvio Quadrifoglio SUV** for about £70,000 – but If I was paying this price I think I might instead sacrifice 150bhp in performance and opt instead for a brand new **Maserati petrol Levante** with a Ferrari engine at around the same cost.

So I am currently arranging test drives for the various models and for the sake of completeness I've also been out in a few rivals, some that might surprise you, as I am plainly not up to date in what you get for your money with a new car. So I am benchmarking the Alfa as follows:

- **New Jeep Wrangler** – a bit quirky and lots of great colours. Verdict – what a stinker to drive, no oomph, noisy and industrial in comparison to even my old Alfa. I wasn't a fan. Good deals on second hand but depreciates quickly.
- **Lexus IS 300H F Sport** – a hybrid petrol and electric saloon with similar performance to the Brera. Verdict – what an astonishingly accomplished drive train this car has, and it looks a bit like a cousin of the Guilia. Sadly a bit plasticky inside and an almost unusable sat-nav / communication system. Shame, a good car at a good price (Circa £35,000 new), my daughter hated it.
- **Porsche Macan 3.0 Turbo diesel** – a smaller SUV at slightly better prices. Verdict – bit boring style wise both inside and out but a very smooth powerful drive. Mrs H wasn't a fan. Prices from just £30,000 for a decent used model.
- **Maserati 3.0 Turbo Levante** – Stunning inside and almost as nice to drive as the Porsche. It's in the running at between £45,000 for a used diesel and £75,000 for a new petrol.
- **Vauxhall Insignia** 1.5 Turbo Tech Line – only a 162 bhp saloon so you may be wondering why this

£23,000 car made the list. Two reasons – I'd recently seen the Australian version on TV being used as an Executive Saloon provided for all Members of Government down-under (and you know already that I used to be a fan of Vauxhalls) – and secondly, in cream it had one of the **plushest interiors** I've seen on any car. So I put it to the test. Verdict – sadly, the car looked unimpressive externally in black and the salesman wasn't wrong when he said *these cars only sell themselves on the interior*, which was smashing. It didn't help that I thought I was testing an Automatic, hence I stayed in one gear for a 5 mile test drive through a City centre and onto fast by-passes, only to subsequently discover it was a manual and had been in **third gear throughout the test drive**, much to the salesman amazement. No wonder it seemed a little noisy and underpowered – but still wasn't that bad overall. So I may revisit Vauxhall AFTER my next car when I need something a bit more sensible.

- **MG GS Exclusive** – another 1.5 Turbo engine, this time 166 bhp. This car made the cut as when I was working out my motoring costs I arrived at the conclusion that this car might just be the **best value in the UK, per month**, particularly with 0% APR loans. So if I wanted low cost transport in retirement AND leather seats (again in cream) then I needed to test this out for comparison. Like the Vauxhall, but in the correct gear, this was also a little noisy when pushed and a bit underpowered, but all in all not a bad car at all with some interesting features like reclining rear seats. Worth considering in future.

In summary, **Alfa are still a very strong contender** for the fourth vehicle in a row although a wild card has literally just (today) entered the ring....a **Maserati**

**Quattroporte**. It turns out these lovely vehicles have suddenly found themselves on the top 10 UK fastest depreciation list – so an £80,000 car can be acquired for just £20,000 after 36 months. Bargain, if they come with red interiors that is!

# Chapter 19

## Would I recommend an Alfa?

If you've read this far you should by now have a pretty good grasp of how much I like Alfa Romeos – but I'm not just saying that out of some historic love of the brand or its racing pedigree, its association with Ferrari (as you can see on my die-cast model car below. NB. The white patches aren't snow or frost, I used superglue by mistake!)

> **Editor's note** – That also explains the wonky seat!

My enjoyment out of the brand comes from the fact these are **well built cars** (provided they are antique or modern cars post 2000 when I believe Alfa also started poaching **quality** control staff from manufacturers like BMW), a **joy to drive,** and have many unusual **quirks**

in a world sadly full of me-too products where every brand copies another.

I have also had a particularly good ownership experience over almost twenty years and notwithstanding being brave enough to try three different Alfa models, the **worst I have experienced is rain dripping on the cloth seats** (presumably as the GT was designed first and foremost on looks and style, plus for a warm climate like Italy, rather than tested to the nth degree in wet countries like Britain).

Maybe I've been lucky with my experiences – although if my data is anything like accurate, owners do seem to stick around.

NB. The **owners club** have also confirmed to me that often buyers of the newer models are existing members with prior history with the marque.

Because Alfa also provide a lot included in the price on most models, I do consider they represent **good value** for money, particularly if purchasing a well loved used model or negotiating a good **discount** on new. This wont make such a compelling case if you pay the ticket price and stumble into a model that sheds value quickly and you don't keep it for years.

So yes, with some caveats which I will come onto in a moment I **would recommend Alfa Romeo** to anyone who values design, who likes driving or whom just likes something a bit unusual. With less than 100,000 cars in the UK out of 31.6 million, **Alfa drivers are part of a 0.3% club** which is pretty exclusive and is just fine for my tastes.

Given all the other factors I've revealed such as the pedigree, driving experience, value for money (versus everyday boring cars), probable low depreciation and the fact that these are not necessarily counter-balanced with any kind of poor ownership experience, reliability issues or breakdowns then I think I will get off the fence and go a stage further – I wont just recommend that everyone tries an Alfa experience at least once, I will go so far as to say I consider **Alfa Romeo to be one of the best kept secrets in motoring.**

Pretty amazing really given how often the brand gets plugged positively by the likes of Jeremy Clarkson, Richard Hammond and James May to name but a few. I guess it just goes to show **how hard it is to shake off things** like a reputation for residual values and rust – even though the latter hasn't been a problem for decades and Alfa are now probably better protected in this regard than 90% of other vehicles on the roads. NB. French cars also seem to be pretty good too.

# Chapter 20

## Hints and Tips.

Owning an Alfa Romeo might to some almost feel as if it's a guilty pleasure, in reality if looked after well, an Alfa can provide many years of enjoyable, trouble free motoring at costs little different to the norm. In short, it's a **practical buy if not always a practical car to use!**

- Let's take my own Alfa Brera as a real life example across the board. Despite being regarded as a sporty vehicle, so presumably they get driven quite hard versus an average car, Alfa sold 2,885 of these cars in the UK (going back 13 years ago) and yet 8 years later when they stopped selling them, 2,455 were still on the roads – that's 85% left after almost a decade.
- From insurance estimates it appears that around 0.3% per annum might be written off in accidents, **leaving just 0.7% per annum** that have either ended up being classed as statutorily off the road (SORN) due to mechanical issues / repair costs or they have been stolen and shipped abroad. It's a **very low failure rate** per year, I think so anyway.

So what steps can help ensure a good Alfa experience?

- Before buying, **research** the model online and look for any regular issues being mentioned on the Online Forums. This is relatively unusual with the modern cars on offer.
- Have a **lengthy test drive and compare it** to what I would call your normal brand. See for yourself if

the driving experience is different and crucially check it's a comfortable driving position. As an example, I know some Ferraris and Lexus don't suit my shape and in many cars my head touches the roof-lining.

- Negotiate hard with the dealership – aim for a minimum of a 5% discount, if necessarily using Bank finance instead of a lease. But the most important thing is to **calculate the full cost of purchase** after adding together all the fee's, monthly payments and final payments – so look at either the **Total** cost of ownership or divide the total by the ownership period to work out a **true monthly cost** as this is never revealed by any car brand or dealership and legislation doesn't appear to enforce it.
- If you can, I think it's **best to purchase from a main dealer** (and get a warrantee) but eventually **service the car elsewhere.**
- Get to **know the dealership service staff** well, so if it's a new car, talk to them whilst the car is under warrantee and try and find out who will actually be looking after your car. So make **excuses** to talk to the people doing the work – don't just settle talking to the receptionist booking the car in. This relationship will hold you in good stead as the Alfa ages.
- If buying a used car outside of any warrantees probably best to avoid using the main dealers for any servicing (unless you already have the kind of relationship detailed above) as the costs will be high. Try and find a **smaller garage** with a clear passion for cars and a willingness to take the trouble to learn about the quirks of Alfas rather than just a bucket-shop quick fix.

- Always have servicing and repairs completed **promptly** at the agreed service schedule periods.
- Only use **quality parts and consumables** such as oil, as these are essential to the car running well. I suspect much of an Alfa's sophistication under the bonnet derives from lessons learned the hard way by the likes of Ferrari on the race track, albeit dumbed down and years later, but you can't imagine them making-do with low cost oil from the pound shop or even Halfords own brand. If you can, stick to the OEM recommendations in the owners handbook.
- Check for a **valid service history** in the service book and keep this up to date so unlike me you can recall if your cam-belt was replaced on time. Better still, keep all the receipts.
- If you get any **strange noises etc, get them looked at quickly** before a more serious fault develops. I would personally focus more on noises than warning lights – I have been told more than once by a main mechanic to just drive on and ignore any lights, or switch the car on and off a dozen times to reset things, and this has been with both Alfa and Aston Martin where the problems did vanish so nothing was actually wrong!
- So if it's a warning light error I would suggest don't panic and dash straight to the garage to get a big unnecessary bill, wait and see if it resets itself – they often do, saving you a fortune. NB. If the car is under warrantee it's worth getting it seen promptly, if you can face the hassle.
- Unless you are a skilled mechanic I would suggest **not cutting corners and trying to do anything yourself** beyond bodywork, in fact, not even that as I reveal in my final chapter!

- Stick to the **recommended tyres and wheel settings.**
- If you want to save money, consider seeking services such as Insurance (or good garage recommendations) from the **Owners Club.**
- When it's time to part with your Alfa, try and sell **privately**. When it was finally time to sell my beloved Brera this pretty much doubled my money.

And that's about it – There is really **nothing a lot more onerous to Alfa ownership than remembering to get tasks properly done** on time and find somebody competent to do so, using good materials.

# Chapter 21

## Summary

Modern Alfa Romeos really are very good cars and I am convinced they are something of a best kept secret.

Despite almost all the motoring press and TV celebrities praising the brand and generally singing the marques praises, they haven't yet worn down the publics reserve, caused presumably by many years of justifiable bad reputation when Alfa Romeo produced a plethora of mediocre cars that rusted, broke down, and on occasion looked downright ugly in the 80's and 90's.

In true Italian style, Alfa have focussed on what they do best – style and engineering innovation, and this is what you get in a modern Alfa, in spades. So if you want a car that looks great and is fun to drive, there is not much on the market to compare IMHO.

And far from the assertion on the book title that you might benefit from being brave if you persist in purchasing an Alfa, this remains as a belief amongst non-owners. The truth is, you don't need to brave at all as you have a more likely scenario of enjoying just as peaceful and event free motoring life as the purchaser of any standard boring box made by run-of-the-mill manufacturers.

And it by no means certain that your wallet or purse will suffer either. If my experiences are typical, and they may just be if my estimates of repeat usage (and my reading of experiences in the owners forum) are accurate – these may be highly engineered vehicles but they don't seem much more likely to cause problems than anything else. The one caveat of course being that using OEM parts may cost a bit more than own brand sold in supermarkets or accessory shops.

Only around 0.3% of UK car owners drive an Alfa Romeo – this is a figure that stacks up well versus the number that drive luxury brands like Maserati or even the 0.06% who drive an Aston Martin, as I did until recently. In each case you are in a fairly exclusive club – but what I find amazing is that the cost to join the Alfa club is only around 20-40% of the expense of joining the other brands, dependent of course on which models you pick. But the gizmos and luxury supplied my not be so different, in short, you could be getting a third of the exclusivity for just 20% of the cost, so surely these are under-priced over-specified cars?

As examples, look closely at the pictures below (sadly in black and white to keep the costs of this book lower for you) and can you easily spot the difference between say an Alfa 156 and a Maserati Levante?

Or maybe a Maserati and an Alfa Brera?

If we also believe the mechanics comments that are also over-engineered under the skin, to me it seems clear they are one of the remaining rare bargains in motoring. So if you want a car that's good to look at, fun to drive, different from the neighbours and has a bit of personality, you can't go far wrong with Alfa Romeo (probably!).

For me, Alfa is a brand I think I can live with for life as it suits my own somewhat quirky personality and I have no desire whatsoever to follow the crowd towards sensible German brands that dominate the world – but from what I have heard with friends cars, they've experienced just as many problems, if not more than I have, with my succession of Alfas.

Whilst their passengers may have had a better experience as said cars will be more practical to get in or out of, easier to park or at the very least they can read the dashboard to see how fast you are driving, my passengers get none of that. The experience in an Alfa is mostly about the driver, and that's ultimately why I like owning one.

Sure for £30,000 or thereabouts I could probably pick up a more involving and even better engineered car like a used Honda Civic Type R boy-racer, but if you want a bit of glamour and luxury in your life and a bit of continental style and panache, I can't honestly think of a better car to buy than an Alfa Romeo which perfectly marries together quality, style and value.

It's a mix that will either fit your personality like a glove or not, if you prefer the more certain route of a teutonic brand it's probably not for you, but if you live for your cars, it probably is about time you were tempted by an Alfa Romeo. How can you disagree with cars like this around......I couldn't!

Brera image courtesy BestCarMag.com

So Alfa Romeo for Brave Alfa Males? No, just cars for drivers with passion and for mechanics with the passion and patience to understand them!

# Footnote

In the end I decided I didn't like the shape of the Alfa Stelvio nor the limited interior options on a Giulia Quadrifoglio . .

> *so my new car turned out to be a Maserati Levante Gran Lusso. It's a lovely car and drives well but much to my surprise even with a top end model it has less gadgets and gizmos than a Giulia 280 which is almost half the price. so with hindsight i may have made the wrong choice and my assertion that Alfa Romeo could just be the best kept secret in motoring, and great value if you buy well and run the cars for years, is a more than accurate conclusion.*
>
> *The Maserati does share many of the Alfa unusual quirks, but the price difference for a posh badge is probably an unjustifiable premium IMHO.*

I now have a further update from November 2019 as due to a series of unfortunate events I've ended up selling the Brera privately, netting £3,000 for a 12 year old car – so its retained over 10% of its original value which surely by any measure other than against classic cars is a more than credible performance?

## So what happened?

The above mentioned purchase of a Maserati Levante 3.0 Turbo Grand Lusso (with full red-leather interior of course) wasn't without problems! I was staying loyal to the Italian theme as promised and thought I was buying a car that was just 8 months old and yet discounted £24,000 versus the price when new.

However the dealers (who will remain nameless as we have agreed out-of-court compensation) failed to do obvious things like clean the new car or repair obvious damage. They also sold me a car that was in fact 4 months older than claimed (and 4 months older than shown at the DVLA) and hence had 4 months less warrantee – these two facts combining to mean I was overcharged by around £1,500 as there are tools to work this out online!

- What I surprisingly discovered is that a warrantee runs from the date the car leaves the factory, not unreasonably, but this date can be very different from when the car is registered with the DVLA and sold. At an extreme example somebody could order a specific specification, it gets made, delivered to the country of origin but if the buyer drops out it may sit unregistered for a year in a field somewhere.

Needless to say I didn't know so it's therefore vitally important to say to your car dealer (and they expected me to do this) "OK, you tell me the car was made in July but when was it _really_ made?". Honestly, who knows this stuff? And all this only became apparent when checking warrantee paperwork supplied after the deal was done!

NB. This gaff cost the dealers an extra year's warranty as compensation and as they say, you live and learn, I won't fall for this salesman's trick anytime soon.

So with the new Maserati as my luxury car I was now planning to keep the Brera as my run-around car and potentially run it into the ground, literally, plus of course try and keep costs to a minimum. But a few things went awry straight away.

- First up I hit a small pothole in a car park entry in Northampton which demolished one corner of the

car's suspension. My mechanic advised fixing both sides for safety reasons. I then decided to also do the front as the handling wasn't the same and I wanted the car to be perfect. So that's circa £750 more spent than expected or necessary.
- I then had a service and MOT done and decided to splash out on a new cambelt (just in case the mechanic was mistaken that it was already OK) and of course with a new water pump needed at the same time this took my bills up to £1,250.
- With so much spent it then made sense to fix three dings (not bad in eight years ownership) and get the car back to showroom condition. I'd always been good at bodywork but hadn't realised with age, skills and eyesight can deteriorate – so it took 4 goes and half the summer to get things up to an acceptable standard ready for spraying.
- Painting also required about 5 goes and £100 in paint and polish costs and to be honest was a complete disaster – the area sprayed got larger each time and the new paint was simply impossible to get a shine on. It needed to go into the Bodyshop but I was too embarrassed to reveal such poor workmanship to them!
- The next unfortunate event was that we happened in passing to mention to my father-in-law that "next time you're considering selling your Vauxhall Corsa, let us know as we might be interested". Emphasis being on the word might.
- This was because his cars are well looked after and very low mileage ( a 3 year old car with just 5,000 on the clock) and yet he always sells before the MOT is due, so we said we'd help him do a "better deal than just selling to the dealer as normal". My wife and I thought it might happen in say a year's time by which point I might be ready to change the

Brera if circumstances have changed? We were already experiencing elderly relatives struggling to get in, despite the huge doors, presumably due to it being a low car.

Anyway, literally just four hours later he contacted us and said "*I've done it*" – he'd gone straight to the local Vauxhall dealership and bought a new car (just the same as the old one but for twice the price!) so we could have his old one for £500 more than the garage offered. (TBH we'd planned on paying the same price so he could negotiate a cash discount but it was rude to haggle).

So now I have three cars and have no choice but either sell my beloved Brera or upset my father in law and refuse to take the Corsa – it's the high powered 90 BHP 1.4 version! Or sell it on immediately, probably for a loss as on the car buying sites it's worth less than we paid and yet we've even had to pay £300 more to get it through an MOT and service immediately!

So I very reluctantly I put the Brera onto Autotrader and was immediately contacted by an interested buyer who liked the unusual specification and paid a £100 deposit for me to hold it as he had to travel 100 miles to see the car at the next available weekend. I was honest in the advert and mentioned the poor paint finish but he agreed to buy the car and a deal was done. He did make mention of the bodywork and then mysteriously couldn't get the cash together to proceed despite shaking hands three times on the deal, I have no idea whether this was genuine or due to things like hassles selling his own existing car or he just couldn't get the cash together in the cold light of day but the deal promised just didn't happen even though he said by text he was still interested. This is of course the downside to selling privately, frustration, but at least the advert was paid for.

I decided to commit yet more money to the car and booked the Alfa into the body shop to fix my handiwork, this way it would be perfect if I kept it or sold it again later. £500 later all my bodged paintwork had been fixed and the car looked almost like new – it would of course have been cheaper to go this route originally than bother with a DIY approach. So plan A was back on, keep the Alfa as it looked like a new car outside and in. If this book was in colour I could show you, it looked a million dollars outside and in as in effect the garage had done more than paintwork, they'd detailed most of the car!

I'd paid the top fee of £75 to Autotrader to run my advert forever until sold and I decided it was time instead to switch tactics and sell the Corsa on. I cheekily asked Autotrader if I could swap my car details over as I needed to sell a different car and keep the original (I could change the photographs and description over to the Corsa but not the heading which was set at Brera), they refused and didn't even offer a discount on a second advert which I think was a little mean. So I placed a free advert for the Corsa on **Motors.co.uk**. At least they are helpful.

That went live in a few days on the next Saturday but before I could take the Alfa advert offline I was contacted by a new potential buyer (having turned previous ones away due to the aforementioned deposit being paid) who wanted to come immediately on Friday night on his motorbike – this time a mere 70 miles, but in the freezing cold and pitch black dark from Essex, so he came to view the car at 7pm on a winter's night. I told him he was crazy but that's 33 year olds for you – enthusiastic!

A deal was struck at £2,900 (down from the advertised £3,100) but with the deposit of £100 being forfeited earlier I'd in effect made my target of £3,000. This was the second cheapest Brera in the country (only beaten by one with 60% more mileage on the clock) so I think a bargain. I'd done OK too as whilst I'd been offered I think £1,850 by the Vauxhall garage a year earlier and £1,000 by the Maserati garage (who really didn't want it) if I added in my £1,850 recent costs, I was getting my money back and had enjoyed the last year's motoring effectively for free, it was just a shame I hadn't had the bodywork done at the start of the year and not the end!

In summary it was a good deal for everyone and will be even better if I can sue the local council for negligence re that pothole which kicked everything off.

So I'm now the proud owner of a 1.4 Corsa with 90 BHP and no oomph instead of a 2.4 Alfa Turbo with 201 BHP, lots of oomph and a glorious leather interior. On the plus side, I kept my Alfa Registration A7FVA so expect to see the Alfa ownership journey continue when I'm tempted back into this marque again, which I will be.

You may be wondering how all this has impacted my final ownership calculations?

- Across my 9 years or Brera ownership my total cost has now reduced slightly to **just £327 per month** (from £340) and the cost per mile is virtually unchanged at 56.5p per mile.
- Interestingly the increased ownership period has meant that I kept this last Alfa for exactly the same time as my super 156 and that overall I have retained my Alfas for 77 months compared to just 44 months for my cars overall.

- Depreciation on the Alfas has finally worked out at just **12.4% per annum** versus 13.5% overall, so putting to bed hopefully the old theory that these cars are difficult to own and you need to be brave!

So that's the end of the Alfa journey, for now anyway.

## Stuart Haining

## December 2019

## Bite-Sized Lifestyle Books

Bite-Sized Lifestyle Books are designed to provide insights and ideas about our lives and the pressures on all of us and what we can do to change our environment and ourselves – and to celebrate life and success.

They are deliberately short and easy to read, helping readers gain a different perspective or develop new interests and experiences. They are firmly based on personal knowledge and where relevant successful actions.

Whether it is about a new skill or introducing new ideas into people's lives – the aim is to make them the *antidote to* **unread** *books* by making them easy to read, challenging and thought provoking – and usually optimistic.

They can be read straight through at one easy sitting or read and pondered over – but most of all they are written for enjoyment.

# Bite-Sized Books Catalogue

## Business Books

Ian Benn
> Write to Win
>> How to Produce Winning Proposals and RFP Responses

Matthew T Brown
> Understand Your Organisation
>> An Introduction to Enterprise Architecture Modelling

David Cotton
> Rethinking Leadership
>> Collaborative Leadership for Millennials and Beyond

Richard Cribb
> IT Outsourcing: 11 Short Steps to Success
>> An Insider's View

Phil Davies
> How to Survive and Thrive as a Project Manager
>> The Guide for Successful Project Managers

Paul Davies
> Developing a Business Case
>> Making a Persuasive Argument out of Your Numbers

Paul Davies
> Developing a Business Plan
>> Making a Persuasive Plan for Your Business

Paul Davies
> Contract Management for Non-Specialists

Paul Davies
> Developing Personal Effectiveness in Business

Paul Davies
: A More Effective Sales Team
: : Sales Management Focused on Sales People

Paul Davies
: The Naked Human in Business
: : Accelerate Your Personal Effectiveness by Understanding Humans – The Practical One Two Three of Business Development

Tim Emmett
: Bid for Success
: : Building the Right Strategy and Team

Nigel Greenwood
: Why You Should Welcome Customer Complaints
: : And What to Do About Them

Nigel Greenwood
: Six Things that All Customer Want
: : A Practical Guide to Delivering Simply Brilliant Customer Service

Stuart Haining
: The Practical Digital Marketeer – Volume 1
: : Digital Marketing – Is It Worth It and Your First Steps

Stuart Haining
: The Practical Digital Marketeer – Volume 2
: : Planning for Success

Stuart Haining
: The Practical Digital Marketeer – Volume 3
: : Your Website

Stuart Haining
: The Practical Digital Marketeer – Volume 4
: : Be Sociable – Even If You Hate It

Stuart Haining
: The Practical Digital Marketeer – Volume 5
: : Your On-going Digital Marketing

Stuart Haining
: Profitable Partnerships
: : Practical Solutions to Help Pick the Right Business Partner

Stuart Haining
- MLM 101
  - The Difficult Questions and Answers Most Networkers Daren't Reveal

Stuart Haining
- The Great Pension Pantomime
  - It's All a Scam – Oh Yes It Is – Oh No It Isn't

Christopher Hosford
- Great Business Meetings! Greater Business Results
  - Transforming Boring Time-Wasters into Dynamic Productivity Engines

Ian Hucker
- Risk Management in IT Outsourcing
  - 9 Short Steps to Success

Alan Lakey
- Idiocy in Commercial Life
  - Practical Ways to Navigate through Nonsense

Marcus Lopes and Carlos Ponce
- Retail Wars
  - May the Mobile be with You

Maiqi Ma
- Win with China
  - Acclimatisation for Mutual Success Doing Business with China

Elena Mihajloska
- Bridging the Virtual Gap
  - Building Unity and Trust in Remote Teams

Rob Morley
- Agile in Business
  - A Guide for Company Leadership

Gillian Perry
- Managing the People Side of Change
  - Ten Short Steps to Success in IT Outsourcing

Art Rain
- The Average Wage Millionaire
  - Can Anyone Really Get Rich?

Saibal Sen
> Next Generation Service Management
>> An Analytics Driven Approach

Don Sharp
> Nothing Happens Until You Sell Something
>> A Personal View of Selling Techniques

# Lifestyle Books

Anna Corthout
> Alive Again
>> My Journey to Recovery

Anna Corthout
> Mijn Leven Herpakt
>> Kruistocht naar herstel

Paul Davies (Editor)
> Still Crazy About George Eliot After 200 Years
>> A Joyful Celebration of Her Novels and Her Writings

Phil Davies
> Don't Worry Be Happy
>> A Personal Journey

Phil Davies
> Feel the Fear and Pack Anyway
>> Around the World in 284 Days

Stuart Haining
> My Other Car is an Aston
>> A Practical Guide to Ownership and Other Excuses to Quit Work and Start a Business

Stuart Haining
> After the Supercar
>> You've Got the Dream Car – But Is It Easy to Part With?

Bill Heine
> Cancer
>> Living Behind Enemy Lines Without a Map

Regina Kerschbaumer
   Yoga Coffee and a Glass of Wine
      A Yoga Journey
Gillian Perry
   Capturing the Celestial Lights
      A Practical Guide to Imagining the Northern Lights
Arthur Worrell
   A Grandfather's Story
      Arthur Worrell's War

## Public Affairs Books

David Bailey, John Mair and Neil Fowler (Editors)
   Keeping the Wheels on the Road – Brexit Book 3
      UK Auto Post Brexit
Eben Black
   Lies Lobbying and Lunch
      PR, Public Affairs and Political Engagement – A Guide
Paul Davies, John Mair and Neil Fowler
   Will the Tory Party Ever Be the Same? – Brexit Book 4
      The Effect of Brexit
John Mair and Neil Fowler (Editors)
   Oil Dorado
      Guyana's Black Gold
John Mair and Richard Keeble (Editors)
   Investigative Journalism Today:
      Speaking Truth to Power
John Mair and Neil Fowler (Editors)
   Do They Mean Us – Brexit Book 1
      The Foreign Correspondents' View of the British Brexit
John Mair, Alex De Ruyter and Neil Fowler (Editors)
   The Case for Brexit – Brexit Book 2
John Mair and Steven McCabe, with Neil Fowler and Leslie Budd
   Brexit and Northern Ireland – Brexit Book 6
      Bordering on Confusion?

John Mair, Richard Keeble and Farrukh Dhondy (Editors)
> V.S Naipaul:
>> The legacy

John Mills
> Economic Growth Post Brexit
>> How the UK Should Take on the World

Christian Wolmar
> Wolmar for London
>> Creating a Grassroots Campaign in a Digital Age

# Fiction

Paul Davies
> The Ways We Live Now
>> Civil Service Corruption, Wilful Blindness, Commercial Fraud, and Personal Greed – a Novel of Our Times

Paul Davies
>> Coming To
>>> A Novel of Self-Realisation

Victor Hill
> Three Short Stories
>> Messages, The Gospel of Vic the Fish, The Theatre of Ghosts

# Children's Books

Chris Reeve – illustrations by Mike Tingle
> The Dictionary Boy
>> A Salutary Tale

Fredrik Payedar
> The Spirit of Chaos
>> It Begins

Printed in Great Britain
by Amazon